THE new FUNK & WAGNALLS
ILLUSTRATED
WILDLIFE ENCYCLOPEDIA

VOLUME 1
AAR-AMO

GENERAL EDITORS: Dr. Maurice Burton and Robert Burton

CONSULTANT EDITOR: Mark Lambert   PRODUCTION: Brenda Glover
DESIGN: Eric Rose   EDITORIAL DIRECTOR: Nicolas Wright

Portions of this work have also been published as The International Wildlife Encyclopedia,
Encyclopedia of Animal Life, and Funk & Wagnalls Wildlife Encyclopedia.

Funk & Wagnalls

DB a company of
The Dun & Bradstreet Corporation

Cover Photo: Tiger
Gordon Langsbury—Bruce Coleman Ltd.

Frontispiece: Waved Albatross
Eric Hosking

ISBN 0-8343-0035-4
Library of Congress Catalog Card Number 80-66926

Printed in the United States of America

Volume 1

Aardvark

African mammal with a bulky body, 6 ft long including a 2 ft tail, and standing 2 ft high at the shoulder. Its tough grey skin is so sparsely covered with hair that it often appears naked except for areas on the legs and hind quarters. The head is long and narrow, the ears donkey-like; the snout bears a round pig-like muzzle and a small mouth. The tail tapers from a broad root. The feet have very strong claws— four on the front feet and five on the hind feet. The name is the Afrikaans for 'earth-pig'.

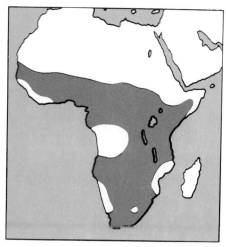

Distribution and habits

The aardvark has powerful limbs and sharp claws so it can burrow into earth at high speed. This it does if disturbed away from its accustomed burrow. There are records of it digging faster than a team of men with spades. When digging, an aardvark rests on its hind legs and tail and pushes the soil back under its body with its powerful fore feet, dispersing it with the hind legs.

The normal burrow, usually occupied by a lone aardvark, is 3–4 yd long, with a sleeping chamber at the end, big enough to allow the animal to turn round. Each animal has several burrows, some of them miles apart. Abandoned ones may be taken over by warthogs and other creatures.

Years can be spent in Africa without seeing an aardvark, although it is found throughout Africa south of the Sahara, except in dense forest. Little is known of its habits as it is nocturnal and secretive,

though it may go long distances for food, unlike other burrowing animals.

Termite feeder

The aardvark's principal food is termites. With its powerful claws it can rip through the wall of termite nests that are difficult for a man to break down even with a pick.

Its method is to tear a small hole in the wall with its claws; at this disturbance the termites swarm, and the aardvark then inserts its slender 18 in. tongue into the hole and picks the insects out. It is protected from their attacks by very tough skin and the ability to close its nostrils—which are further guarded by a palisade of stiff bristles.

As well as tearing open nests, the aardvark will seek out termites in rotten wood or while they are on the march. It also eats other soft-bodied insects and some fruit, but—unlike the somewhat similar pangolin, which has a muscular, gizzard-like stomach filled with grit for crushing hard-bodied insects—it cannot deal with true ants.

Breeding cycle

The single young (twins happen occasionally) is born in midsummer in its mother's burrow, emerging after two weeks to accompany her on feeding trips. For the next few months it moves with her from burrow to burrow, and at six months is able to dig its own.

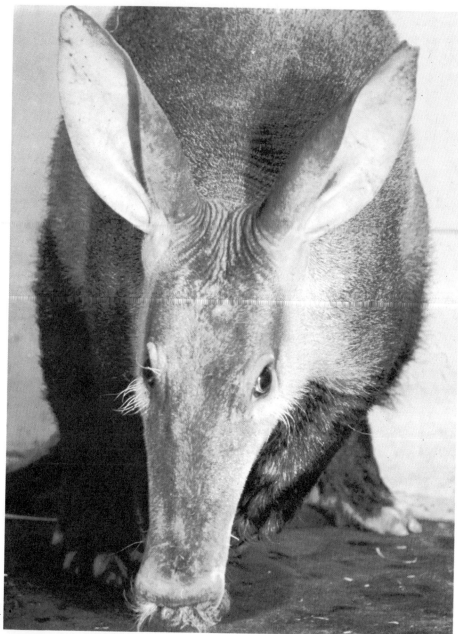

▷ *The aardvark's nose is guarded by a fringe of bristles and it can also close its nostrils, as a protection against termites.*

Okapia

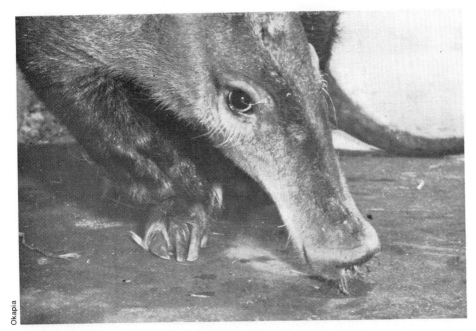

Digs to escape enemies

The aardvark's main enemies are man, hunting dogs, pythons, lions, cheetahs and leopards, and also the honey badger or ratel, while warthogs will eat the young. When suspicious it sits up kangaroo-like on its hind quarters, supported by its tail, the better to detect danger. If the danger is imminent it runs to its burrow or digs a new one; if cornered, it fights back by striking with the tail or feet, even rolling on its back to strike with all four feet together. On one occasion, when an aardvark had been killed by a lion, the ground was torn up in all directions, suggesting that the termite-eater had given the carnivore a tough struggle for its meal. However, flight and—above all—superb digging ability are the aardvark's first lines of defence for, as with other animals with acute senses like moles and shrews, even a moderate blow on the head is fatal.

A creature on its own

One of the most remarkable things about the aardvark is the difficulty zoologists have had in finding it a place in the scientific classification of animals. At first it was placed in the order Edentata (the toothless ones) along with the armadillos and sloths, simply because of its lack of front teeth (incisors and canines). Now it is placed by itself in the order Tubulidentata (the tube-toothed) so called because of the fine tubes radiating through each tooth. These teeth are in themselves very remarkable, for they have no roots or enamel.

So the aardvark is out on an evolutionary limb, a species all on its own with no close living relatives. Or perhaps we should say rather that it is on an evolutionary dead stump, the last of its line.

What is more, although fossil aardvarks have been found—but very few of them—in North America, Asia, Europe and Africa, they give us no real clue to the aardvark's ancestry or its connections with other animals.

class	**Mammalia**
order	**Tubulidentata** *sole representative*
family	**Orycteropidae**
genus & species	***Orycteropus afer***

◁ *The wall of a termite nest is so hard it is difficult for a man to break down even with a pick-axe but the powerful claws of the aardvark can rip through it easily.*

The termites are so disturbed by having their nest opened that they swarm about and the aardvark then puts its pig-like muzzle into the nest to eat them.

It has an 18 in. long, slender, sticky tongue with which it captures and eats the swarming termites that make up the main food of aardvarks.

▷ *A day-old aardvark. It depends on its mother for six months until it can dig its own burrow. The aardvark's snout and round, pig-like muzzle earn it the Afrikaans name for 'earth-pig'.*

Aardvark escape route

Disturbed away from its burrow, the aardvark can escape its enemies by digging at incredible speed. It forces the soil back with its fore feet and kicks it away with its strong hind legs, 'so fast that it can outstrip a team of six men with spades'.

Aardwolf in its rock crevice lair. It spends the day here and comes out at night to feed.

Des Bartlett: Photo Res.

Aardwolf

African member of the hyaena family, differing from the true hyaenas in having five instead of four toes on the front feet, relatively larger ears, and a narrower muzzle. Also, the jaws and teeth are weaker than those of the true hyaenas.

The body, somewhat larger than that of a fox, weighs 50–60 lb. The coat is yellow-grey with black stripes, except for the legs, which are black below the knee. The muzzle is black and hairless, the tail bushy and black-tipped. The hair along the back and neck is long: this ridge of hair usually lies flat, but when the animal is frightened it erects the hair around the neck—or, in extreme cases, along the whole back.

The name is Afrikaans for 'earth-wolf'.

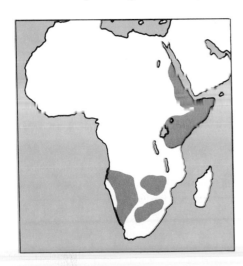

Distribution and habits

The aardwolf ranges throughout southern and eastern Africa as far north as Somalia. It is nowhere common but is found most frequently in sandy plains or bushy country.

It is rarely seen, since it is a nocturnal animal and spends the day lying up in rock crevices or in burrows excavated in the soil. The burrow consists of two or more sharply winding tunnels 25–30 ft long, leading to a sleeping chamber about 3 ft in diameter.

Termite feeding hyaena

The aardwolf lives almost entirely on termites and other insects, but lacks claws strong enough to tear open termite nests, so it is limited either to picking up the insects from the surface of the ground, or digging them out of soft soil. The speed and efficiency with which the long tacky tongue sweeps up insects was impressively shown when the stomach of an aardwolf that had been run over was opened up. It contained some 40,000 termites, although the aardwolf was unlikely to have been foraging for more than three hours. This gives an average consumption of at least three termites per second.

When insects are in short supply, the aardwolf may turn to other prey; mice, small birds and eggs of ground-nesting birds are the main victims. Eating carrion has been reported, but it is more likely that the aardwolves were feeding on the beetles and maggots within the carcasses.

Breeding cycle

A single litter of two to four is born each year, in the southern part of the range in November-December. The gestation period ranges from 90 to 110 days. The young are born blind.

Mistaken persecution

The aardwolf's main enemy is man, who tends to kill them in mistake for hyaenas, for which bounty is paid in many areas. Despite their rigid protection by the London Convention for the Protection of Fauna in 1933, the aardwolves have suffered persecution in farming country, both through mistaken identity and the idea that they take poultry.

The natural enemies of the aardwolf are probably the same as those of the aardvark —pythons, lions and leopards.

For defence, aardwolves can put up a good fight with their long canine teeth and can eject an obnoxious, musky fluid from their anal glands.

Insect-eating carnivores

Aardwolves resemble hyaenas sufficiently for them to be shot by mistake, yet at one time they were classed as a separate family, the Protelidae. Now they are considered to be members of the Hyaenidae but forming a separate genus, *Proteles*.

The reason for the separation from the true hyaenas is their insectivorous habits. For although they have fewer adaptions for feeding on termites than aardvarks—weak claws and no palisade of bristles guarding eyes and nostrils—the aardwolves still show considerable differences from their carnivorous relatives. The hyaenas are hunters and carrion eaters, with powerful neck and jaw muscles and strong teeth. The aardwolf's teeth, by contrast, are a sorry sight. Apart from the fairly large canines, they are ridiculously small, and the cheek teeth are few in number. An aardwolf's skull gives the impression of an animal having died of old age and worn-down teeth.

class	**Mammalia**
order	**Carnivora**
family	**Hyaenidae**
genus & species	***Proteles cristatus***

Abalone

Several species of molluscs related to the limpets. Also known as ormer, sea ear, or earshell, the abalone (four syllables, the final e being sounded) somewhat resembles a snail, the body being little more than a muscular foot with a head at one end, bearing a pair of eyes and sensory tentacles. The body is also fringed with tentacles.

Along the side of the shell is a line of holes, through which water is exhaled after it has been drawn in under the shell and over the gills to extract oxygen. New holes are formed as the shell grows forward, while the old holes become covered over, so that only a few younger holes are open at any one time, the rest appearing as a line of bumps.

Some abalones are among the largest shellfish: they range in size from the 1 in. long and very rare Haliotis pourtalese to the red abalone of California, which is up to 10 in. across.

Helmut Stellrecht

Jane Burton

D.P. Wilson

△ *Abalone showing edge of foot and its frill of tentacles which seek out its seaweed food.*

◁◁ *Mother of pearl, used in making jewellery, lines the inside of the abalone shells.*

◁ *A black abalone without the encrusting seaweeds which grow on most other species.*

▽ *The starfish is one of the abalone's main enemies. It uses its hundreds of sucker feet to prise the abalone away from its rock. The starfish then turns its stomach inside out and pushes it beneath the abalone's shell to dissolve away its flesh.*

Distribution, habitat and habits

Abalones are to be found in many parts of the world: along the coasts of the Mediterranean, Africa, Australia, New Zealand, the Pacific islands, and the western coast of North America. In the Atlantic they are found as far north as St. Malo and the Channel Islands. The rare species *Haliotis pourtalese* is found off Florida. It is known mainly from specimens washed up on the shore, as it lives at depths of 350–1,200 ft. It is thus the deepest-living of all abalones; the rest live between the extreme low-water mark and a depth of about 60 ft along rocky shores where there is no sand to clog the gills or in rocky pools large enough not to be heated too quickly by the sun. The only other exception is the black abalone, which lives in the splash zone where waves breaking against rocks alternately cover and expose it.

Unlike their limpet relatives, abalones have no 'home', no spot on a rock where they always return after feeding. They simply hide up in a crevice or under a rock, avoiding the light and coming out at night. When disturbed an abalone grips the rock face, using its foot as a suction pad: the two

Helmut Stellrecht

main muscles of the body exert a tremendous force—up to 400 lb in a 4 in. specimen. Unlike the limpet, the abalone cannot bring its shell down over the whole of its body: the edge of the foot, with its frill of tentacles, is left sticking out.

Abalones move in the same way as limpets and snails. Waves of muscular contraction pass along the foot, pushing it forward. As each part expands it is fixed to the ground by slimy mucus: the part in front, expanding

in turn, is pressed forward and then itself stuck down. Abalones differ from limpets and snails in having a sort of bipedal movement. Alternate waves of movement pass down either side of the foot, so that as a part of one side is moving the corresponding part on the other side stays fixed.

The rate of travel is very rapid for a shellfish: a speed of 5–6 yd/min has been recorded—although no abalone would cover this distance in one dash.

△ *The abalone breathes through the line of holes along its shell. As it grows, new ones form and others are covered over.*

▽ *The remarkable teeth of a radula, the mollusc tongue, magnified 1,450 times by using a deep field scanning electron microscope.*

E.S. Hobson

Many-toothed tongue for feeding

Abalones are vegetarians, crawling over rock faces and browsing on seaweeds that they seek out with their sensitive tentacles. Their favourite foods are the delicate red weeds and green sea lettuces, although they also scrape tissue off fragments of kelp that have been torn away by waves. Young abalones eat the forms of life that encrust rocks, such as the coral-like plant *Corallina*.

Food is scraped up and chewed into small pieces by the rasp-like action of the radula, a tongue made up of large numbers of small, chalky teeth.

100,000 eggs laid

Some molluscs are hermaphrodite but all individual abalones are of one sex or the other. They reach sexual maturity at six years. The germ cells, or gametes, are shed directly into the sea, causing great wastage. Thus a female will liberate 100,000 or more eggs, and the sea around a male turns milky

over a radius of 3 ft when he sheds his milt. To reduce wastage, however, the female does not shed eggs until induced by the presence of sperms around her.

The fertilised eggs are covered by a gelatinous coat and float freely in the sea until they hatch a few hours later as minute trochophore larvae. These trochophore larvae are top-shaped and swim around by means of a band of hair-like cilia around the thickest part. Within a day the trochophore develops into a veliger—a miniature version of the adult complete with shell but still with the band of cilia. Two days later it loses the cilia, sinks to the bottom and starts to develop into an adult, a process that takes several weeks.

The free-swimming larvae have advantages in that they are the means by which the otherwise rather sedentary abalones can spread, but they are very vulnerable and are eaten in their millions by plankton-eating fish like anchovies and herrings.

Enemies everywhere

Although mortality is heaviest during the free-swimming stage, adult abalones also have several enemies. Fish, sea birds, sea otters, crabs and starfish dislodge the abalones or chew bits off them. Their only protection lies in their tenacity in clinging to rocks and the protective camouflage of the shell and foot. This camouflage is improved by the seaweeds and sedentary animals that settle on the shell. Also, it has been found that when young abalones feed on red weeds their shells become red.

On the other hand abalones are more vulnerable due to the boring sponge *Cliona lobata*, which erodes holes in their shells and so opens them up to other predators. In the Channel Islands as many as 95% of a sample of abalones have been found to be infected with boring sponges.

Dark pearls, called blister pearls, are sometimes found in abalones. Like the real pearls of oysters, these are formed by the animal to cover up a source of irritation—in this case a minute parasitic clam, *Pholadidea parva*, that bores through the abalone's shell and into its tissues.

Prized for shell and meat

The shells of abalones are prized because, although they are superficially rough and dull, cleaning reveals the gleam of mother of pearl. This and the large size of the shell make abalones popular with shell collectors, and they are also used for making costume jewellery. The body itself is much esteemed as food. The large foot is cut into strips, beaten with a mallet to make it soft, and then fried. The edge of the foot is trimmed off to make chowder.

The popularity of abalones and the ease with which they can be collected from the shore has led to stocks being severely depleted. In California, which is the centre of the abalone industry, only strict laws have prevented its extinction. As abalones do not breed until they are six years old and perhaps 4 in. long, there is a minimum length at which they can be taken: for the common red abalone this is 7 in., corresponding to about 12 years of age. There is a close season—though it now seems that abalones breed all the year round—and catches are limited to five a day and can only be taken by a licence-holder.

Finally, abalone meat cannot be exported from the State of California. This does not mean, however, that it cannot be obtained outside California, as tinned abalone meat is exported from Mexico and Japan, and many most of the abalone eaten in the United States are imported from Mexico.

phylum	**Mollusca**
class	**Gastropoda**
subclass	**Prosobranchea**
order	**Archaeogastropoda**
family	**Haliotidae**
genus & species	*Haliotis rufescens (red abalone)* *H. fulgens (green abalone)* *H. cracherodii (black abalone)* others

Accentor

The name of 12 species of small, rather sparrow-like birds forming a single genus and family. They differ from sparrows in having slender and finely pointed bills and a well developed tenth primary wing feather. They are generally regarded as being related to the thrushes or the warblers.

Two accentors are found in Europe. One, the dunnock or hedge sparrow (but not in fact a sparrow at all) is a rather featureless bird, identifiable by the grey on its breast, neck and head and its dark brown wings. Its song, which can be heard virtually all the year round, is a hurried jingle rather reminiscent of that of the wren.

The other European species is the alpine accentor. This is a larger bird, more brightly coloured than the dunnock; it has a whitish bib spotted with black and conspicuous white-bordered chestnut feathers on the sides of the body.

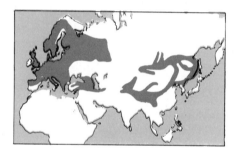

Habits and habitat

Accentors are found throughout Europe and Asia. The dunnock can be seen all over Europe except in parts of the far north and south. In Britain it is common wherever there is suitable habitat except in the north, where it becomes rarer—it is seldom seen in the Shetlands.

The alpine accentor is found on mountain ranges from Spain to Japan, extending down to North Africa. Occasionally individuals wander into Britain.

The typical habitat of accentors is in mountainous regions, often well above the tree line and up to the snow line. The Himalayan accentor is found breeding as high as 17,000 ft above sea level, and one race of the alpine accentor breeds up to 18,500 ft above sea level. However, most species breed in the scrub vegetation at rather lower levels. Some species are hardy enough to spend the winter at high altitudes, but others migrate downwards. The remainder live in forests. The dunnock is to be found in many kinds of habitats, but especially in gardens, hedgerows, copses and scrubland.

Accentors are quiet and unobtrusive, remaining close to the ground in the undergrowth. If flushed they fly low and in undulating fashion to cover. On the ground they proceed by leisurely hops or a kind of creeping walk, with the body almost horizontal. The wings are often flicked in a

characteristic manner—this is most noticeable in the dunnock during courtship and has earned it the name of shuffle-wing.

Most species in the accentor's family, the Prunellidae, tend to live together in flocks. The dunnock, however, is usually a solitary bird, coming together in small groups only for feeding and a peculiar wing-flicking display. There is little migration—it is mainly just from higher to lower ground and from far north to south. Vagrants of the alpine accentor, however, have reached

Eric Hosking

In England, the fast-disappearing hawthorn hedge is a favourite nesting site for the dunnock, or hedge sparrow. The female makes the nest from leaves, twigs, moss and grass. The male plays no part in nest building or incubation.

the Faroes, and the Siberian accentor has turned up in Alaska.

Insects in summer, seeds in winter

During the summer months accentors are insectivorous, eating spiders and insects such as beetles, butterflies and flies. In winter they live almost entirely on seeds and berries, even picking them out of animal droppings. They have a finch-like crop and muscular gizzard, and swallow grit to help in breaking up the seeds.

Breeding

The males sing from rocks or low bushes, sometimes making short, lark-like song flights. Among dunnocks the male plays no part in building the nest or in incubation. The female makes the nest in a rock crevice or in a shrub, out of leaves, twigs, moss and grasses, sometimes with a few feathers (dunnocks very occasionally use a lot of feathers for the lining). Sometimes an old blackbird's or swallow's nest is used. The nest is cup-shaped, and five dark blue eggs are laid in it. The hen incubates for about 12 days, leaving the nest only to feed. In species other than the dunnock the male shares in nest-building and incubation.

The young are fed by both parents and fledge in about 12 days. Those of the alpine accentor sometimes leave the nest before they can fly. Dunnocks have two and sometimes three broods a year.

Sings in all seasons

In musical parlance an accentor is one who takes the leading part in singing. We should therefore expect birds called accentors to be outstanding either for their song or for some other feature. In fact they are all relatively inconspicuous birds—the name 'dunnock' refers to the dun plumage. They tend to live in inaccessible places and also to make great use of cover.

Nor is the song of an accentor particularly loud or distinguished. But it is persistent. The dunnock, for example, has a short, high-pitched song that is heard at all seasons, by night as well as by day. It is most constantly and vigorously repeated when the bird is excited, as when two rival males meet or the birds are courting. The dunnock is evidently a very light sleeper and will respond to the slightest disturbance at night with a snatch of melody: you can hear it sing in the bush as you pass, especially if you shine a torch towards it. It will also respond by singing to a sudden gust of wind or a scud of rain. Although the breeding season is not particularly early in the spring, the dunnock's courtship begins in December and its song gains vehemence at that time when the weather keeps most birds more silent than usual.

John Markham

△ *The red lining in a young dunnock's mouth stimulates the parents to drop food in. Parents will 'feed' imitation mouths if they are red.*

▽*One race of the alpine accentor has been found as high as 18,500 ft above sea level, feeding on insects caught in mountain air currents.*

Richard Vaughan

class	**Aves**
order	**Passeriformes**
family	**Prunellidae**
genus & species	*Prunella modularis* (dunnock) *P. collaris* (alpine accentor) 10 other species

Addax horns, curving out from the base and spiralling over the back, are considered the most graceful of any animal's. They can reach nearly 1 yd in length and are so prized by hunters that the addax is now very rare.

Addax

A single species in the antelope family, closely related to the oryxes. Also known as the screwhorn antelope, it differs from most antelopes in the absence of facial glands and in the large square teeth, which are more like those of cattle.

An adult male standing some 40 in. at the shoulder weighs about 250 lb. The colouring of the coat varies with the season: in winter it is greyish brown with white hind quarters, underparts and legs; in summer the body becomes sandy or almost white. The head is white and distinctly marked with brown and black patches to form a white X over the nose. Between the horns is a tuft of long black hairs, and there is a short mane on the neck. The tail is short and slender, tipped with a tuft of hair.

Both sexes bear horns, the female's being somewhat thinner. The horns are like those of the oryx but curve out from the base and spiral back over the neck. A length of nearly 1 yd, measured in a straight line from base to tip, with 1½–3 spiral turns, may be attained.

Habitat

At one time the addax extended across the Sahara from the Atlantic coast to Egypt, particularly in the sand-dune areas. The ancient Egyptians kept it in at least semi-domestication: pictures in a tomb dating from 2000 BC show addax and other antelopes wearing collars and tethered to stakes. It seems also that the number of addax a man owned was an indicator of wealth and position. Certainly the addax would have been among the most beautiful of status symbols.

More recently, addax were to be found from Algeria to the Sudan, but never farther south than a line drawn roughly from Dakar to Khartoum. Now they are much restricted and becoming increasingly rare: numbers are estimated at about 5,000. They are still found in Algeria, Niger, the Sudan and Chad with a concentration in Mauretania and Mali. Precise details of captive addax are recorded in a stud book held at San Diego Zoo, USA. During 1966 and 1967, in seven zoos throughout the world, 33 offspring were bred and in 1974 there were 146 captive addax around the world.

There have been two causes of this reduction. First, their habitat is being destroyed by the opening up of desert areas for commercial projects, in addition to the destruction of its sparse vegetation by herds of domestic goats. Secondly, the addax themselves are being killed by hunters. The horns are considered the most graceful of any animal's—a sure cause of persecution—and the hide is used for shoe leather. The addax is slow by comparison with other antelopes, so it falls an easy prey to man and his dogs. It is not difficult to ride an addax to exhaustion, for it will panic and use up its energy in a blind attempt to maintain a high speed. A mounted hunter following at a gentle trot will exhaust an addax after an hour, and modern hunters in cars can 'blow' one in less than ten minutes. The animal is then so exhausted that it can hardly attempt to defend itself.

In the Sudan, however, the addax's chances of survival are now improving, because the nomads who had been the cause of the reduction in numbers are settling in more hospitable areas away from the addax's haunts. Yet it was only in 1966 that the addax was given formal protection—not that this will be easy to put into practice. One factor meanwhile that enhances its chances of survival is its adaptation to a desert habitat. The hooves are short and widely splayed, enabling it to travel over the sand in the rapid journeys that are a feature of desert animals that have to cover large areas in search of scanty supplies of food.

Moreover, the addax is able to survive in the very depths of the desert where conditions are so extreme that no other warm-blooded animal can survive permanently. Although it can drink large quantities of water at a time, the addax is nevertheless able to survive without any free water almost indefinitely, sufficient water being obtained either from succulent vegetation or from dew that condenses on plants.

Habits

The addax's habits are not well known, owing to the thinly spread and inaccessible nature of the population. Addax are very wary; at the slightest alarm they dash off at a frantic gallop. If disturbed too often they may travel so far as to lose themselves in the more arid parts of the desert and die of starvation. In 1963 a camel patrol found addax spoor and, nearby, a fresh uninjured carcass of an addax that had apparently died thus.

Sensitivity to disturbance is increased by the addax's extreme sensory powers. These are well developed, as in many desert animals that live far apart and that would otherwise have difficulty in locating each other.

Typically, addax move about in small troops of 4–20 animals—rarely more than 30—led by an old male. Very occasionally, herds of as many as 300 have been seen. Normally the troops stay in one area, providing there is enough vegetation. Otherwise they may move long distances.

Staple diet of grass

The movements of addax are intimately related to the distribution of their food, which in turn is related to the weather. They are most likely to be found along the northern fringe of the tropical summer rains, moving north in winter as the Mediterranean trough system brings rain southwards. The addax can tell where the rains have fallen by scenting from a distance where the vegetation has turned green.

The staple diet is the *Aristida* grasses, perennials which may be green throughout the year, reacting to humid air or rain as the weather belts pass by. These plants are sensitive even to a single shower of rain, sprouting and remaining green all winter.

Addax are fastidious feeders, eating only certain parts of a plant. When feeding on the *Aristida* grasses they crop all the blades to a level height. On the other hand the outer, dried blades of *Parnicum* grass, the favoured food of the southern addax, are not touched. They take only the fresh green blades, pushing their heads into the middle of the clump, gripping the growing stems and breaking them off with an upward jerk of the head. *Parnicum* seeds are also very much favoured. They are plucked by drawing the stalk through the mouth so that all the seeds are cleaned off. As the seeds are present throughout most of the year and are rich in protein they form a valuable item of the addax's diet.

Addax droppings are always covered by a thin layer of mucus. It has been suggested that some of the leguminous plants eaten by the addax secrete viscous fluids which in turn cause the addax to secrete mucus from the walls of the intestine. This mucus layer eases the passage of the rough vegetation and will prevent the dry stalks from taking up water at the addax's expense.

The shy desert living addax is now very rare because it is ruthlessly hunted, but at the San Diego zoo addax are being bred in captivity.

Breeding unknown

Almost nothing is known about the addax's breeding except that one young is born at a time, usually in winter or early spring. In captivity, at least, the calf is born when the mother is 2-3 years old after an 8-9 month gestation.

They beat the censor

During the Second World War, servicemen abroad had their letters censored. But the urge to let their people at home know where they were seems to have been irresistible. Or perhaps it was no more than a kind of game, to beat the censor. At all events the methods and means used in the attempt were diverse and ingenious.

The censors were also cunning, and quite often a letter reached its destination with little of its contents intact. But one piece of information was passed by the censor and succeeded in giving astute families an idea of where the sender was stationed. American soldiers wrote home describing a 'white antelope'. Armed with this description their families went to zoos and got the animal identified. The white antelope was the addax—this meant the North African campaign.

class	**Mammalia**
order	**Artiodactyla**
family	**Bovidae**
genus & species	***Addax nasomaculatus***

Popperfoto

Adder

A snake, member of the viper family. The adder has a relatively stout body for a snake and a short tail. The average male is 21 in. long, the female 2 ft —the record length is 2 ft 8 in. The head is flat, broadening behind the eyes to form an arrow-head shape.

The colour and body-markings vary considerably; adders are among the few snakes in which male and female are coloured differently. Generally the ground colour is a shade of brown, olive, grey or cream; but black varieties in which all patterning is obliterated are fairly common. The most characteristic marking is the dark zig-zag line down the back with a series of spots on either side; the head carries a pair of dark bands, often forming an X or a V.

It is often possible to distinguish the sex of an adder by its colour. Those which are cream, dirty yellow, silvery or pale grey, or light olive, with black markings, are usually males; females are red, reddish brown or gold, with darker red or brown markings. The throat of the male is black, or whitish with the scales spotted or edged with black; females have a yellowish-white chin sometimes tinged with red.

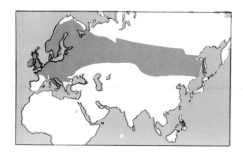

Distribution and habits

The adder ranges throughout Europe and across Asia to Sakhalin Island, north of Japan. In the British Isles it is absent from Ireland and the northern isles but is the only snake found in Scotland. It is usually to be seen in dry places such as sandy heaths, moors and the sunny slopes of hills where it often basks in the sun on hedge-banks, logs and piles of stones. It is, however, also found in damp situations.

Its tolerance of cold allows the adder to live as far north as Finland, within the Arctic Circle. It escapes cold weather by hibernation, which starts when the shade temperature falls below 9°C/49°F. It emerges again when the air temperature rises above 8°C/46°F—even coming out on to snow— but a cold spell will send it in again. The duration of hibernation depends, therefore, on climate: in northern Europe it may last up to 275 days, whereas in the south it may be as little as 105 days. In Britain, adders usually hibernate for about 135 days in October-March, depending on the weather.

Unlike many other snakes adders do not burrow but seek out crevices and holes

Geoffrey Kinns AFA

△ The adder's tongue looks menacing but is harmless. It is a smell-taste organ, picking up particles from the air and withdrawing them for analysis in the mouth.

▽ The hedgehog is one of the adder's enemies. It is protected by its spines while it alternately bites and rolls up, until the adder is dead.

where they lie up for the winter. The depth at which they hibernate depends, like duration, on the climate: in Britain the average depth is 10—12 in., but in Denmark, where winters are more severe, adders are found at depths of 4 ft.

Very often many adders will be found in one den, or hibernaculum. As many as 40 have been found coiled up together, along with a number of toads and lizards. This massing together is a method of preventing heat loss, but it is not known how the adders come to congregate in the hibernacula, which are used year after year. It may be that they can detect the scent left from previous years.

It is uncertain whether adders are nocturnal or diurnal. Their eyes are typical of

A black adder. Adders range in colour from cream, through dirty yellow to silvery grey or olive (male); and from red to gold (female).

nocturnal animals in that they are rich in the very sensitive rod cells: such eyes will see well at night, but during the day they need protection, and the adder's slit pupils cut down the intensity of light. On the other hand, despite these adaptations, adders are often active during the day. Courtship and some feeding are definitely diurnal; the timing of the latter depends on how hungry the adder is.

Rodent killer
The adder's main prey is lizards, mice, voles and shrews. Young adders subsist at first on insects and worms. Larger victims are killed by a poisonous bite, the effects of which vary with the size of the prey. A lizard will be dead within a few minutes, or even within 30 seconds; but an adder's bite is rarely fatal to humans.

The adder's method of hunting is to follow its prey by scent, then poison it with a quick strike of the head. While the poison acts, the victim may have time to escape to cover, in which case the snake will wait for a while then follows to eat its dead prey.

Dance of the adders
The mating period is from the end of March to early May, though it has been known to last until autumn. In the north of Europe the summer is too short for the eggs to mature in one year, so breeding takes place in alternate years.

At the beginning of the breeding season, there is a good deal of territorial rivalry

between males, culminating in the 'dance of the adders'. Two males face each other with head erect and the forepart of the body held off the ground. They sway from side to side, then with bodies entwined each attempts to force the other to the ground by pushing and thrusting. They do not attempt to bite each other.

Finally one gives up and departs. The female, who is frequently waiting close at hand, will accept any victorious male, if she is ready, and a male will mate with any female. He crawls up behind her and loops his coils over her body, rubbing his chin (which has especially sensitive skin) on her back until he reaches the back of her neck, and mating takes place.

Adders are ovoviviparous: that is, the eggs remain inside the mother's body until they are fully developed, and the young are born coiled up in a membrane which is ruptured by their convulsive movements. They have an egg tooth, which in other animals is used to rupture the egg membranes, but in adders it is degenerate as they have no need of it, and the tooth is so situated that it is of no use for this purpose. It is shed a few days after birth.

The young are born in August or September and the number ranges from five to 20: 10-14 are most common, each measuring 6-8 inches in length. They are immediately capable of independent existence, but often they appear to stay with the mother.

△ Male (left) and female adders are always differently coloured.

▽ Adder with day-old young.

The adder has no external ear or ear drum, but picks up vibrations from the ground through its lower jaw. The vertical slit pupil gives quick perception of horizontal movement.

Predators defy poison
Like most animals—even those well capable of defending themselves—adders are most likely to flee if confronted with danger, and they usually bite only if suddenly frightened. But, despite not having the excuse of self-defence, man is their chief enemy. However, the killing of adders on sight has not led to their decline, although nowadays increased urbanisation is destroying their habitat.

Undoubtedly many carnivores will take adders. Foxes and badgers kill them, and they have been found in the stomachs of pike and eels. Surprisingly, perhaps, the hedgehog is a great adversary of adders: one reason is that it can tolerate large doses of venom without harm. Its method of killing is to bite the adder, then curl up leaving nothing but a palisade of spines for the snake to strike at. It repeats the process of biting and curling until the snake is dead, after which the hedgehog eats it.

A confusion of names
The Anglo-Saxon name for the adder was *naedre*, which became 'a nadder' or 'a nedder' in Middle English. Later the *n* was transposed, so that we now have 'an adder'. The alternative name viper comes from the Anglo-Saxon *vipere* or *vipre*, itself derived from the Latin *vipera*. This was a contraction of *vivipara*, from *vivus* (alive) and *parere* (to bring forth)—alluding to the animal's method of reproduction. In general 'viper' was used to mean any venomous snake. There being only one such snake in England, viper and adder became synonymous for the one species (viper also being used to describe a venomous or spiteful person).

The two words have spread with the English language all over the world, being used not only for snakes of the genus *Vipera*. There are the near relatives such as the gaboon viper, more distant, like the pit vipers and mole vipers, and the death adder, which is not even in the viper family.

class	**Reptilia**
order	**Squamata**
suborder	**Serpentes**
family	**Viperidae**
genus & species	***Vipera berus***

Adélie penguin

Penguins are found in Antarctica, but not the Arctic, and are not, as is often thought, restricted to the frozen land and sea. Various species of penguin live around the coasts of South America, Africa and Australasia, usually not going far north but staying where the sea is still quite cool. The Peruvian penguin can be found right along the coast of Chile and Peru, where a cold current of water sweeps up towards the Equator. The Galapagos penguin lives even on the Galapagos Islands, just on the Equator, where the sea is surprisingly cool.

With the emperor penguin, the Adélie is confined to the Antarctic continent and its neighbouring islands. Other species, including the chinstrap, gentoo and macaroni penguins, live around the fringes of the continent and on the islands; but their main breeding grounds are farther to the north, in sub-Antarctic and temperate latitudes.

The penguin is a flightless gregarious bird; a superb swimmer, it is beautifully adapted to life in water; the wings having evolved into flippers, and the body become covered with a protective layer of blubber. Its progress on land seems comically clumsy when compared with the efficient grace with which it moves through the water.

Many penguins have distinctive colouring around the head, sometimes with plumes or crests of orange feathers. But the Adélie penguin, which stands about 18 in. tall, is simply coloured, with a white belly and black back and throat. The eye is distinguished by a surrounding circle of white that gives the bird the appearance of a golliwog.

The penguin is a flightless bird, its wings having evolved into flippers.

Antarctic environment

On a September or October day on the edge of the Antarctic continent, with the sea frozen as far as the eye can see, quite suddenly, a line of dots might appear, moving in a straight line across the ice. Each dot seems to be gliding along as if pulled by a string, until it reaches a crack in the ice when some of the dots suddenly change shape. A closer inspection would show them to be Adélie penguins which have been tobogganing over the ice on their bellies, using their feet and flippers to propel themselves. When they reached the crack they stood up to get a better view across it. After a bit of jostling they walk to the edge of the crack, waddling on their ridiculously short legs, and holding out their flippers for balance. Eventually they jump across and resume their slow progress.

These penguins are on their way to the nesting grounds, or rookeries, where they nest in thousands. They have spent the long winter on the edges of the frozen seas where there is an abundance of food and they are now in prime condition, their bodies padded with half an inch of blubber and their feathers sleek and glossy. At first the groups consist of a dozen or so penguins, but they increase in numbers until streams of penguins are flowing in towards the rookeries.

From rookery to creche

At the rookery, which is usually situated on a rocky headland, each penguin searches for its old nest, or if it is breeding for the first time, finds an empty space. The nests are still covered with snow, but the penguins know exactly where to look for them. The males usually arrive first and they stand on the nest, fighting off other males and waiting for their mates. They have a special display that at once intimidates other males and attracts females. It is called the 'ecstatic display': the penguin points his bill to the sky, waves his flippers to and fro and utters a loud braying call.

When all the penguins have arrived and the pairs have formed it can be seen that each penguin sitting on its future nest is exactly the same distance from each of its neighbours. This even spreading ensures that they do not interfere with each other too much and that the eggs and chicks will not be disturbed. Occasionally a penguin does get in the way of its neighbours and a fight breaks out. Penguins fight by pecking and by beating with their flippers.

When the snow melts, nest-building can begin. The male collects pebbles which he takes one at a time to the female, who remains standing on the nest site. He drops each pebble in turn at her feet and she uses them to build up a ring around her. Usually the pebbles are laboriously collected from the beach, but the penguins miss no chance to steal them from any unguarded nest.

Two white eggs, each 2 in. long, are laid in the nest of pebbles; the male broods them while the female goes back to the sea to feed—for she will not have eaten for two or three weeks. A fortnight later she returns, while the male goes off to break his fast of some six weeks, during which he will have lost almost half his weight. The eggs hatch after 36 days and for the first few days the chicks stay under their parents.

While one parent is guarding the chicks the other collects food for them, returning with it stored in the crop where it is partly digested. Reaching the nest, the adult penguin opens its beak to the chick. The chick then pushes its head into the adult's mouth to take the food that is disgorged.

The chicks grow rapidly, coming out from under the parents to stand by the nest. Then, when a month old, they leave the nest to gather in groups called *crèches,* from the French word for public nurseries. It was once thought that the adult penguins that stood around the crèches were special guardians, looking after the chicks while the parents were away feeding; but it is now known that they are birds that have lost their eggs and are just standing around.

Once the chicks have joined the crèches the adults do not simply walk up and feed them. Instead they lead the chicks away from the crèche, making them run over the rocks and then make their way back again after they have been fed. One function of this is to introduce the chicks to the outside world, for soon they will be leaving the crèche and taking to the sea.

▷ *Two penguins leap out of the water to join their companions on the ice-covered shore.*

Lewis Smith

▽ *Adélie penguins tobogganing over the ice on their bellies, using feet and flippers to propel themselves.*

Lewis Smith

ewis Smith

△ *Nests are built by the female from pebbles brought by the male, and each pair has its own nest territory, evenly spaced from the next. This penguin 'rookery' includes a pinkish 'erythristic' Adélie and a pair of chinstrap penguins.*

Anthony

▷ *Month old Adélies leave the nest to live in crèches.*

Crustacean feeder

It is at first sight surprising to find colonies of thousands of penguins in the apparently desolate wastes of the Antarctic; but in contrast with the land, the Antarctic seas are teeming with life—especially with the small shrimp-like creatures such as amphipods and krill on which the penguins, as well as the seals and whales, feed. The reason for this abundance of food lies in the circulation of the oceans. Moving southwards toward Antarctica, there is a current that flows along the ocean beds. In it are the salts, such as phosphates and nitrates, that are brought down to the seas in rivers and are also released when dead animals from the surface layers sink and decompose. On reaching the cold Antarctic this warm current, rich in nutrient salts, wells up to the surface and the salts nourish myriads of minute planktonic plants. These in turn nourish the small animals on which the penguins feed.

Skua and leopard seal enemies

There are no land animals in the Antarctic to menace the rookeries, but predatory sea birds, the great skuas, breed near the rookeries, and take the eggs and chicks of the penguins whenever the opportunity arises. They wait for a penguin to neglect its eggs for a second and swoop down to carry one away in the bill. Sometimes a pair of skuas will work together, one attracting the penguin's attention while the other sneaks up behind to steal an egg. Later, the skuas wait around the crèches for a chick to become separated from its fellows. The skuas are unable to kill a healthy chick but can harass a weakened one until it succumbs.

Both adults and the young are in danger from leopard seals as they enter the water. Again a healthy alert bird will probably be safe from them and the seals have to be content with chasing weakly penguins.

Selfish and callous?

There is a story of Adélie penguins which seems to credit them not only with a high level of intelligence but with a selfishness

C.Herbert: British Antarctic Survey

▷ *Adélie penguins are gregarious birds living on the Antarctic continent and its neighbouring islands.*

▷ *An Adélie penguin stands 18 in. high.*

Russ Kinne: Photo Res.

that is rivalled only by the most callous of humans. The story as usually told is that the penguins will go to the edge of the ice, line up along it and then push one of their number into the water. If that one comes to the surface again all go in, because they then know there are no leopard seals about. If the unfortunate one that has been ducked does not surface, they know a leopard seal has eaten it and all turn round and walk away, postponing their fishing until later.

On the face of it this seems too extraordinary a story to swallow, and yet it has been reported again and again even by serious zoologists. It seems the story was brought back by the early Antarctic explorers and particularly by Ponting, the

photographer on Scott's expedition to the Antarctic, who lectured widely on his return.

A simpler explanation is much more likely. When a crowd of penguins are walking across the ice and come to an obstacle, for example, a wide crack in the ice, all will stop and inspect it. There is a good deal of jostling, and any penguin that is pushed to the edge tries to get away and run round to the back of the crowd. They may even do the same if they come to a hump in the ice. After this exploration one of them will in due course jump across the crack and the others stream after it: penguins tend to behave like a flock of sheep and will stand around until one of them starts moving.

It is easy to see that if this sort of thing

happened at the edge of the ice a penguin might go into the water of its own volition: but it might look as if it had been pushed. Anyone seeing this, who did not have the advantage of the increased knowledge of penguins and of animal behaviour that we have today could very readily misinterpret what he had seen.

class	**Aves**
order	**Sphenisciformes**
family	**Spheniscidae**
genus & species	***Pygoscelis adeliae***

AFGHAN HOUNDS

Many legends and myths abound regarding the origin of the Afghan Hound, and some believe that this was the breed of dog which Noah took with him into the Ark. However, the Afghan Hound as we know it today originated in Afghanistan and very few genuine facts are known about it before the 19th century. A scarcity of historical data on the breed has always been noted. The claim made by a Major McKenzie to have discovered rock carvings depicting Afghan Hounds in caves at Balkh with later inscriptions on them dating back to Alexander the Great, has never been substantiated, as no trace of these caves has ever been found.

The Afghan Hound is a member of the gazehound family (sight hunters) and is commonly known in Afghanistan as Tazi. Two types existed in their native country—the finely boned and sparsely coated plains Afghan and the stockier, heavily coated mountain type. The Afghan Hound was used for both hunting and guard duties and is still highly prized by Afghan tribesmen. Even now outsiders will find it difficult to acquire an Afghan—visitors have traced an Afghan puppy and bargained with the owner, only to return the next day and be told the puppies all ran away or died in the night.

The earliest known illustration of an Afghan Hound is dated 1813 and depicts a 'Meenah of Jajurh', a native soldier, with a small, dark-coated Afghan Hound.

Afghans first appeared in Europe at the close of the 19th century, being brought home by English Army officers returning from service on the North West Frontier. In 1907 an Afghan Hound was exhibited by Captain Barff at the Crystal Palace Show where he won the Foreign Dog Class. This was the legendary 'Zardin' who was a well-grown, relatively heavily coated hound with a great personality. He caused such a sensation that Queen Alexandra asked to see this unusual breed of dog and he was 'presented' at Buckingham Palace. 'Zardin' died mysteriously and none of his progeny survived him.

In 1921, Miss Jean Manson and Major and Mrs Bell Murray arrived back in England from India with a number of Afghan Hounds and established the Bell Murray Kennels. In 1925, Major and Mrs Amps returned to England from the North West Frontier bringing with them the Afghans who were to be the foundation stock for the Ghazni Kennels. One of these dogs was the celebrated 'Sirdar of Ghazni' and the majority of modern-day Afghan Hounds in England descend from this famous dog. The breed expanded gradually in England, but after a slight set-back occasioned by the Second World War, numbers grew rapidly until today it has become the most popular breed of dog in the show-ring.

A self-willed breed

Afghan Hounds were first seen in the USA around 1926, coming in from the Southern Seaways, but the breed really 'took off' in 1930 when Mr and Mrs Zeppo Marx (the youngest of the famous Marx Brothers) brought two Afghans, 'Omar' and 'Asra', from England to California. These were sold to Mr O A Shaw McKean, a respected dog breeder, who was one of the early pioneers of the breed in the USA. Their popularity knew

Two regal Afghan Hounds at ease.

J. S. Knight

no bounds and as well as featuring prominently in Best in Show awards, they were used in films and were in great demand by advertising companies. They even gained Obedience CD and UD awards, this being no mean feat as Afghans can be exasperating to train, being a very self-willed breed. Mrs Frank Burger had a troupe of eight Afghans in her twenty dog Burger Circus Act who were trained to do a cake-walk dance and skip with a double rope. The star attractions of the show were two all black Afghans complete with gloves and trunks, slugging it out in a three round boxing match!

Afghan racing

Afghan racing started in England and continued and expanded in the USA and is also a very popular activity among European Afghan enthusiasts. Coursing has also been tried with this breed. An Afghan racing track was built at Massachusetts and racing is run on the same lines as Greyhound racing, complete with muzzles, racing silks and an electric hare. Some comparatively fast times are clocked. Some Afghans thrive on racing, others only chase the hound in front of them, whilst many just clown playfully around the track.

Eastern exotic

The first comparatively short breed standard was drawn up in England in 1925 and was based on the famous 'Zardin'. In 1927, a new fuller and more detailed standard was drawn up and was in force in the breed until 1946, when the British Kennel Club drew up and issued one official breed standard for each breed registered at the Kennel Club. The British official standard is not the only one in the world, although it has been adopted by most European countries. American enthusiasts drew up their own breed standard and this was officially adopted in 1949.

The Afghan Hound is an aristocrat—his whole appearance is one of dignity and aloofness with no trace of plainness or coarseness. He has a straight front, a proudly carried head and eyes which gaze into the distance as if in memory of ages past. The striking characteristics of the breed are exotic or 'eastern' expression, long silky topknot, peculiar coat pattern, very prominent hip-bones, large feet, and the impression of a somewhat exaggerated bend of stifle due to profuse trouserings. These characteristics stand out clearly, giving the Afghan Hound the appearance of what he is, a king of dogs that has held true to tradition throughout the ages.

This head study of a black-masked golden Afghan clearly shows the almost triangular eye shape.

Sally Anne Thompson

Africa

Carol Hughes: Bruce Coleman Ltd.

Africa as Gondwanaland

With its 11 710 000 square miles, the African continent occupies one quarter of all the world's land not covered by water. According to a well defended hypothesis, it has existed since the end of the Palaeozoic era and once formed part of the super-continent of Gondwanaland. (Gondwanaland united Africa, Madagascar, South America, the Indian peninsula, Australia and Antarctica.) This theory explains very well indeed the majority of animal and plant distributions, but is not universally accepted. To be absolutely certain, we must await the progress of physics and submarine geology to tell us more about the movement of the earth's plates. One day, without doubt, chronology founded on radio-active minerals will help us resolve the problems concerning the origin and the exact history of continents; in the meantime we still have an extremely rich harvest of geological (chiefly stratigraphic and palaeontological) data. The same rocks and same fossils are found from one part to another of certain seas, particularly in the Atlantic. Since 1963, palaeomagnetic evidence has resulted in a resurgence of interest in Wegner's original theory of continental drift, which he put forward as long ago as 1915. Today, the study of plate tectonics, or the relative movements between continental and oceanic plates, draws the concepts of sea-floor spreading, continental drift, crustal structures and world patterns of earthquakes and volcanic activity together as aspects of one coherent picture.

An old Pre-Cambrian base

Africa extends for a more or less equal distance either side of the equator in both northern and southern hemispheres. Simple in form, this massive continent is three times the size of Europe – but with less total coastline. Looked at broadly, Africa is a high land which is considered flat, because it lacks particularly high or long mountain ranges, like those of Asia and America. Kilimanjaro is its highest peak and, discounting the Atlas and Ethiopian mountains, and those of southern Africa, it only has isolated ranges. But low plains in Africa are also few and far between. The average altitude of the Sahara is 1300 to 1600 ft above sea level. Going south, the Sudan is already a little higher and covered in part by savanna. Next comes Africa's great southern triangle, which forms a vast plateau situated at 3000 ft and descends in a series of terraces or embankments towards the sea.

To understand Africa's general physiography we need to go back into prehistory. The rocks which form the base of the continent are Pre-Cambrian. They were crushed together on three occasions in long distant times and form chains orientated more or less north to south – or from Ethiopia to the Cape. But erosion has done its work, and Africa has been subjected to a wearing down by denudation. In fact, if this country was well and truly in the centre of a much larger land mass, it is likely that secondary flexures occurred in the Carboniferous period – and new periods of erosion then followed, which resulted in a levelling of the land.

Geomorphology

Each continent has a base, or structural nucleus of ancient and violently deformed granitic rock, which was at the core of primitive mountain systems, though these are not necessarily vestiges of the original terrestrial crust. A typical process would then be that the base became covered with mainland or marine sedimentation – and was made level. The whole might then undergo secondary deformations, resulting in great rays of curvatures and faults; but the first folding had already acquired a granitic rigidity. In Africa, the first covering was clearly crinkled up in this way, while subsequent layers remained sub-tabular. Today, therefore, the African continental base displays great curvatures with scattered rims. The fractures were probably produced in the Tertiary period and created great trenches of subsidence, like the Lake Nyasa region in Mozambique; and trenches of this sort stretch from the Zambesi to the Dead Sea. The Atlas range, which borders on the

According to the theory of continental drift, at the end of the Palaeozoic era, all the continents were united into one huge mass, Pangaea. All the water (except interior seas) became one ocean, Panthalassa.

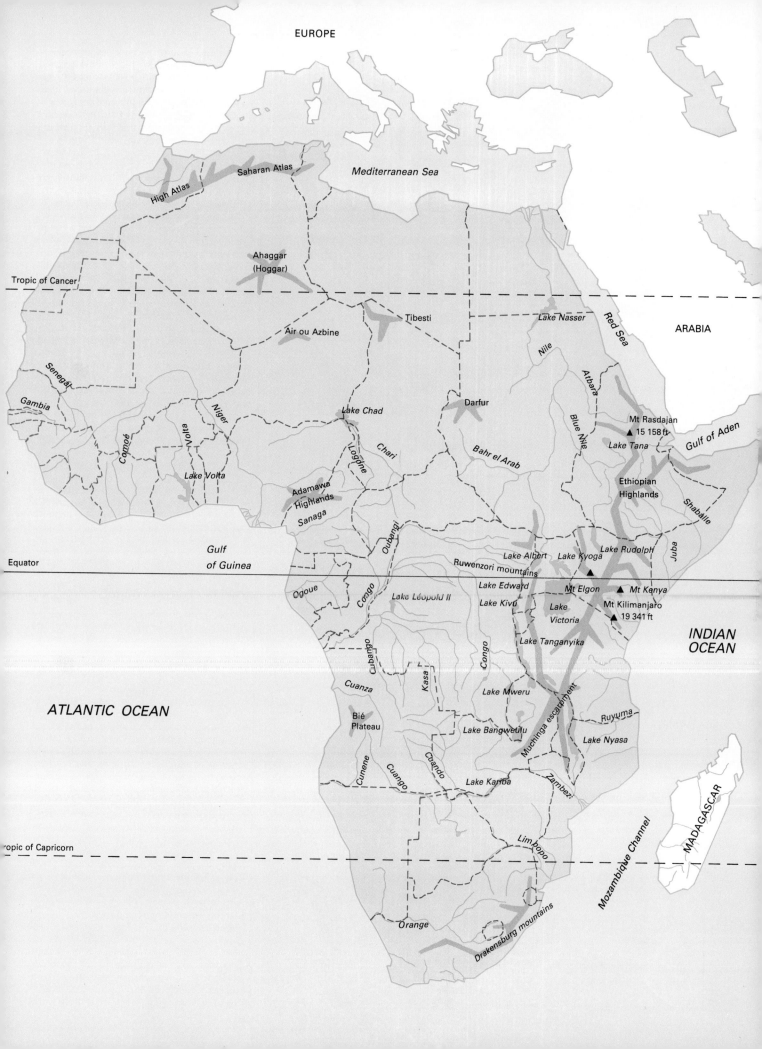

EUROPE

Mediterranean Sea

High Atlas Saharan Atlas

Tropic of Cancer

Ahaggar
(Hoggar)

Tibesti Lake Nasser

ARABIA

Red Sea

Air ou Azbine

Nile

Mt Rasdajan
▲ 15 158 ft

Senegal

Niger

Darfur

Atbara

Gulf of Aden

Gambia

Canoé

Volta

Lake Chad

Chari

Blue Nile

Lake Tana

Ethiopian
Highlands

Shabâlle

Lake Volta

Loggne

Bahr el Arab

Adamawa
Highlands

Sanaga

Oubangi

Lake Albert

Lake Kyoga

Lake Rudolph

Juba

Ruwenzori mountains

Equator

Gulf
of Guinea

Ogoue

Congo

Lake Léopold II

Lake Edward

Lake Kivu

Mt Elgon ▲

▲ Mt Kenya

Mt Kilimanjaro
▲ 19 341 ft

Lake
Victoria

INDIAN
OCEAN

Cubango

Congo

Lake Tanganyika

Kasa

ATLANTIC OCEAN

Cuanza

Lake Mweru

Ruvuma

Bié
Plateau

Lake Bangweulu

Muchinga escarpment

Lake Nyasa

Cunene

Cuango

Cuando

Lake Kariba

Zambezi

Limpopo

MADAGASCAR

Mozambique Channel

Tropic of Capricorn

Orange

Drakensburg mountains

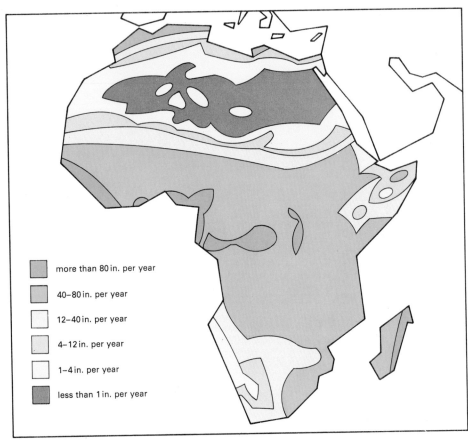

Although Africa has a great variety of climates, it is predominantly tropical, being hot and dry. The rainfall (above) according to region is difficult to show, as it varies with the currents according to season. It follows, then, that the distribution of vegetation (below) is also only an approximation. However, most of the rain falls in the equatorial regions of the continent and this has led to the formation of dense tropical forests. To the north and south there are regions of desert.

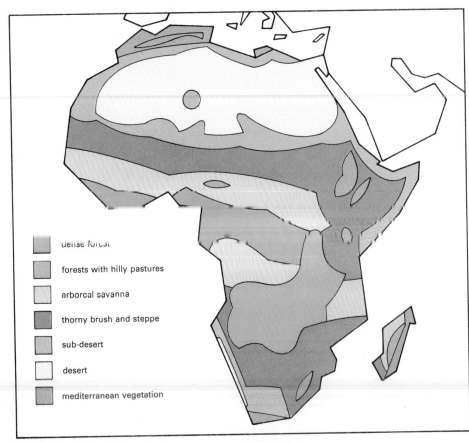

Legend (rainfall map):
- more than 80 in. per year
- 40–80 in. per year
- 12–40 in. per year
- 4–12 in. per year
- 1–4 in. per year
- less than 1 in. per year

Legend (vegetation map):
- dense forest
- forests with hilly pastures
- arboreal savanna
- thorny brush and steppe
- sub-desert
- desert
- mediterranean vegetation

Sahara, was formed in the Tertiary period. In other regions, the fractures were accompanied by volcanic eruptions; these were of different types, but all caused new dislocations. The Karroo in South Africa, for example, is lava-capped. Great volcanic overflow created the devastated Abyssinian plateau, the summits of east Africa, the Cameroons, and mountains of the Sahara like Hoggar. However, in contrast to these initial Pre-Cambrian upheavals, the mountains of countries such as Morocco, Algeria and Tunisia can be related to alpine geology.

In sum, Africa has had to undergo such a process of levelling that the continent can be broadly considered as a single great plain with a disorganized system of rivers and lakes. Certain sections of this great horizontal surface have altered in level and formed basins separated by shelves of land. These basins have permitted the concentration of water and this has given rise to the great African rivers; but of all these territories, only Chad remains totally land-locked, rather like a small inland sea. Immense regions are not drained as they might be, however, and the result is marshlands in rainy periods, and zones totally deprived of water at dry times of the year. The passage of African rivers towards the sea has not been easy either. Everything in the continent depends on very special geographical relief. A watercourse can be navigable over good distances, then suddenly rendered impassable by rapids and cataracts. Despite their size, these rivers are generally quite calm and slow, and have little effect on hard rock – the more so as they are not particularly charged with alluvium, which might hollow out a generally deeper bed.

African climates

In the burning wastes of the Sahara, Africa is the hottest part of the world. But in general it divides into climatic zones in relation to latitude and presents a whole gamut of climates–which are influenced more by rainfall than temperatures. Africa's dominant climate is tropical. An equatorial climate governs the low latitudes of the Congo, the Gabon coast, the southern part of the Cameroons and Nigeria. In the east, however–in Burundi, Uganda and Kenya–the same climate undergoes modification and there is less rainfall than in the west. In Guinea, in the west, the influence of latitude reigns unopposed. But only a little further north, in Nigeria, the rainfall is already less abundant than it is in Guinea.

On the African continent there is relatively little differentiation of geographical relief capable of hindering the penetration of wind. What relief there is, unlike other continents, only manifests itself on the regional scale. Apart from the north and the south, which have a Mediterranean climate, what characterizes the African climate is constant, unrelenting heat, which is either accompanied by extreme dryness or abundant rain.

Looking at the African climate in the general terms of dry, or humid, suffocating heat, explains the appearance of deserts, savannas, or tropical forest. Moreover, a zone of territory will, or will not, be entrenched in direct relation to one or other of these climatic extremes. Naturally, the

EUROPE

Mediterranean Sea

Leopard

Hyaena and jackal

Cheetah

Tropic of Cancer

Chimpanzee

Ostrich

Hyaena and jackal

Crocodile

ARABIA

Red Sea

Gabbon viper

Crocodile

Lion

Giraffe

Giraffe

Elephant

Cheetah

Zebra

Giant eland

Hippopotamus

Aardvark

African buffalo

Chimpanzee

Black rhinoceros

Hyaena and jackal

Giraffe

Chimpanzee

Gulf of Aden

Elephant

Green monkey

Warthog

Leopard

Lion

Okapi

Grant's gazelle

Elephant

Gaboon viper

Pangolin

Dik-dik

Ostrich

Green monkey

Hornbill

Giant eland

Impala

Zebra

Black rhinoceros

Elephant

African buffalo

Hippopotamus

Equator

Gulf
of Guinea

Pangolin

Hyaena and jackal

Gorilla

Ostrich

INDIAN
OCEAN

Gaboon viper

Gorilla

Giraffe

Antelope

Pangolin

African buffalo

Elephant

Giraffe

Cheetah

Ostrich

Giraffe

ATLANTIC OCEAN

Black rhinoceros

Impala

Hornbill

Lion

MADAGASCAR

Warthog

Lion

Zebra

Hippopotamus

Chimpanzee

Elephant

Hyaena and jackal

Mozambique Channel

Tropic of Capricorn

Crocodile

Aardvark

Lion

Leopard

Aardvark

Chimpanzee

Zebra

27

coasts are influenced by cold currents; and the Canaries current in the north, and the Benguela in the south, induce dryness by lowering the temperature. On the Indian Ocean coast the currents alter according to the season: cold currents come from the north in winter, warm from the south in summer. Uniquely, the Mozambique canal has a warm current running all year round. The eastern shorelines are also watered by the trade winds. In the region of the gulf of Guinea, the humid trades that come from the south are in conflict with the mainland trades, while the coasts of Mauritania are already dried by the Canaries current and are unaffected by the monsoon system that waters inland areas.

A great variety of landscapes
The climatologically complex African continent has been said to have the simplest arrangement of vegetation in the world. Parallel zones of vegetation are shown as extending north and south from the equator in fine symmetrical lines. Either side of the equator lies the region of abundant rain–and luxuriant vegetation. Then, still going north and south, the humidity gradually lessens and with it vegetation. There are savannas with less thickly wooded trees and gallery forests (near watercourses); but always according to more or less large parallel cartographic bands. Next there is desert–the

Sahara in the north, the Kalahari in the south. However, overlapping does occur. Africa offers an extraordinary range of intermixed landscapes. Certain zones have been almost destroyed as the result of man's intervention; long-balanced ecosystems have disappeared; sometimes even the soil itself has been attacked and regional climates disturbed. By his use of fire to clear land for cultivation, man has created savannas in areas where they did not exist previously. The initial ecological climax has disappeared in many secondary zones–and even equatorial forest that is cut down takes up to 200 years to reconstitute itself.

The beginning
The way in which the continents were related in prehistoric times permitted the primary distribution of flora and fauna. Over the millennia which followed, these developed in different ways on each separate land mass, but they all retained some common characteristics.

The primary distribution probably came about in the Tertiary period. Africa in the Miocene epoch was certainly luxuriantly forested right up to Arabia and Egypt and probably had a considerable uniformity of fauna. Unfortunately, we have no entirely precise method of determining distribution in those times and therefore cannot be too assertive. We can be sure, though, that

Gondwanaland, which once encompassed Africa, was itself at the time part of a single worldwide continent–Pangaea. Everything in the scientific study of geographical limits demonstrates that such an original immense mass must have existed. Angiosperms, for instance, could not have spread other than in a continued network. Even in atmospheric currents, it is unlikely that their seeds could have crossed the vast stretches of the oceans. So we can safely assume that the original differentiation of flora and fauna first occurred on one immense continent–and endemic species or families were the result of later isolation.

First populations
Climatic and geological upheavals subjected the prodigious richness of the world's original flora and fauna to great, and often adverse, changes. Glaciation, for instance, lowered the level of the sea by as much as 650 ft and new lands appeared. Conditions were modified virtually everywhere to different degrees and the result was a great extinction of life forms that could not adapt. Along with the rest of the world Africa, which had been continental from the very beginning, underwent important climatic modifications. These resulted in altered vegetation and, through that, distribution of fauna–which began to resemble the fauna of the continent today.

The Tibesti Mountains in the Sahara Desert. There are several oases here, particularly in Bardaï.

Extraordinary diversity of animals

The fauna of the African continent is immensely rich and varied and cannot be spoken of in general for, in effect, there is not one Africa but several. The extent of ancient disturbances can never be determined; great zones of territory which border one another can have contrasting fauna, and observations on them sometimes appear quite arbitrary. Without dealing in detail with specific bioclimatic sectors, we intend to start in the northern desert, journey south to the Cape—and examine everything we meet on the way.

Animals of the northern desert and semi-desert

The animals that live in the desert (which originally came from slightly less hostile neighbouring regions) can only survive there by, in some way or other, escaping its most extreme temperatures. They are certainly specialized for life here, but it is doubtful if we can really call this adaptation. No animal, except perhaps the dromedary, is impervious to the full Sahara sunlight and continued existence in the desert is only possible as the result of micro-climates which induce a degree of mildness. Desert vegetation can be ephemeral, the reproductive cycle of a plant being accomplished in some weeks, or months, depending on the species. Usually seeds develop rapidly and germination is ultra-rapid. The plants themselves may dry out and disappear, but their seeds are extremely resistant and, if unable to germinate on maturity, they can germinate with the next rains—even if they are a long time coming.

No life can exist without water, but some animals can 'cheat' on imposed conditions as the situation demands. Many animals are represented in the desert, but few are really *of* it. Their acclimatization in all probability came about progressively in former times when the tropical climate was less arid. The fauna which first penetrated the desert is comparable to that of the Sudanese region today. Even if there is no water at all there for weeks or possibly months, animal life is practically never absent. An animal's ability to travel can sometimes make up for local deficiencies in water. Mammals and birds which already have regular and obligatory migrations can reach it easily. Less mobile creatures burrow into the earth and remain there throughout the day, and with good reason. The Sahara has the highest recorded temperature in the world, 58°C/136°F—in the shade.

Metabolic water

Certain animals are adept at living in the most arid conditions—for example, gerbils (p. 1014). Also known as sand-rats, some of these rodents (of the genera *Gerbillus* and *Meriones* which are specific to the Sahara) do not drink, and exist on food with a water content of only 10%. These gerbils manage to live with a 50% lower than normal humidity. All told, there are some 54 species of *Gerbillus* and 12 of *Meriones*. The thick-tailed mouse *Pachyuromys duprasi* has a store of fat in its tail which measures over 2 in. long—out of the animal's overall length of just 5½ in. This is an exception, however. Other members of the group do not have strategic reserves and economize water by means of their metabolism. As a result, these rodents only lose half the amount of water an ordinary rat does. Concentrated urine and dry excrement are the signs of this faculty of adaptation in which the organism oxidizes food—and so provides the water essential to life.

A nocturnal rhythm of life—in which an animal avoids the heat of the day exactly as it would a dry season—is as important as metabolism. At night, a desert away from the coast has relatively humid air—humid enough, at any rate, for many creatures like sand beetles, which haunt the dunes.

The desert receives 90% of the radiation from the sun, a small part of which is reflected by dust. When most available plants die due to drought, certain animals become more and more sluggish—and so have less need for water. This lethargy occurs among insects and small mammals and we will return to it.

Desert plants

There are 1200 species of plants in the Sahara, some of which survived the drying out of the climate which took place in the Quaternary period. Otherwise, seeds have been carried there from the south or north. A good number of regions, of course, particularly those with stony soil, have no plants at all. But the very extent of the Sahara must be taken into account: to the south its dry season, when the leaves fall, occurs in winter; to the north, under the influence of a Mediterranean climate, the reverse is the case and the dry season occurs in this region in summer.

Rock hyraxes

Water is the determinant factor for all desert animals, and the differences between them are established, in essence, by how well they can manage without it. As water is so indispensable, places that have it are in great demand among desert creatures. But water loss is limited among certain animals by mechanisms of retention and rock hyraxes (*Procavia* spp p. 1286) thrive in the desert. Rock hyraxes are also called dassies or conies. They also live in several other regions of Africa and, as well as the hyraxes of the Sahara, the Abyssinian hyrax and Sudan hyrax are worth mentioning, as they get along equally well in savanna, steppe or desert.

Desert mammals

The wild sheep *Ammotragus lervia sahariensis* of the Sahara is known as the Aoudad or Barbary sheep. It is native to North Africa and is the only wild sheep indigenous to Africa. It is related to the domestic sheep, and is well adapted to the dryness of the desert. Aoudads are found from the Atlantic coast to the Red Sea, and southward to the Sudan and the north bend of the Niger River. Their watering places are sometimes a long way from where they live, but they can survive on the occasional green plant and bush which have been moistened by dew. They are nocturnal by habit, resting during the day.

The scimitar-horned oryx (p. 1774) subsists in the same way, taking advantage of condensation produced on plants during the cooling of the desert at night. A large antelope, it is a close relation of the Arabian oryx, which is on the way to extinction. Both are well adapted to desert regions and can exist without water for weeks. These animals also move considerable distances with the seasons, either towards the interior of the desert or to the south.

With its wide hooves, the addax *Addax nasomaculatus* (p. 15), which was once widespread, is superbly adapted to life on great sand dunes—and to every exceptionally arid region. It unfailingly selects the most tender and succulent shoots of the plants it feeds on—and can survive without water for a very long time. Two gazelles (p. 1005) are also true desert-dwellers: the dama gazelle, which is found throughout the Sahara; and the dorcas gazelle, which lives in stony regions.

Camel and dromedary

The camel (p. 484) is perhaps the most commonly known inhabitant of the desert. Camels are able to withstand great differences in temperature, and although inconvenienced by humidity, they resist dehydration with singular ease. Indeed, the weight of a camel's body can drop by 10% in a dry period without in any way upsetting it. There are two members of the camel family (the Camelidae). The two-humped or Bactrian camel is found only in Central Asia. Here in Outer Mongolia wild herds may survive, but most seen in zoos today are domesticated varieties. The Arabian camel has one hump. It is not completely domesticated—and lives wild in North Africa and Arabia. The dromedary is a domesticated Arabian camel that has been bred for speed and racing. Both species of camels—'ships of the desert'—have helped man penetrate territories he would never have been able to reach on his own. The 'African camel' is, in fact, Arabian, but there are hybrids between Bactrians and Arabians.

Whatever the form of the camel, the hump does not contain a reserve of water. In fact it

Tatera bohemia, one of the many species of gerbils or sand rats. Most gerbils live in the desert and semi-desert regions of Africa.

consists mostly of fat, which the animal uses by breaking it down chemically inside its body to provide it with energy. Only by process of oxidization does this produce a little water. When it gets the chance to, an Arabian camel will drink enormous amounts; but only a small part of what it consumes is retained—in its stomach.

Desert birds

There is life everywhere in the desert—though it is not always discernible. Unlike certain mammals, birds can only exist without water for a relatively short time; but because they can fly they can make up for this deficiency by leaving drought areas in search of water holes or streams. Furthermore, their small size allows some of them to get much of the water they need from dew.

Birds of prey are also found in this region, though in general their presence tends to be sporadic. The lappet-faced vulture *Torgos tracheliotus* is a denizen of great areas of North Africa. Another, smaller bird of prey, the Egyptian vulture *Neophron perconopterus* lives in desert-steppes and deserts, and high in the sky the lanner falcon *Falco biarmicus* can be seen surveying the great reaches of semi-desert. Though not exactly a desert predator, the buzzard largely borders on the specifically North African zone and is worth mentioning. We shall return to other birds of prey later on.

Seed-eaters and insect-eaters

The sand partridge *Ammoperdrix neyi* is found in the north-east of the continent and the small African rock partridge *Ptilopachus* south of the Sahara. A bird well represented here—and everywhere in Africa—is the lark. The desert lark *Ammomanes deserti*, or isabelline, lives in full desert. The thick-billed lark *Rhamphocorys clotbey* lives more to the north in stony deserts, as does the hoopoe lark *Alaemon alaudipes*.

Knowing what birds eat tells us a good deal about them and their life styles. Granivores need places with water. Insectivores can exist without water more easily. The feeding habits of birds can vary too. The thick-billed lark, for instance, catches lizards, which it then dissects before eating.

The bluethroat *Cyanosylvia svecica*, a migratory bird from northern Europe, crosses the Sahara, where many die, like other species, due to the harsh conditions they have to endure. But a group of birds more accustomed to desert regions are the desert wheatears of the genus *Oenanthe* (which actually live in a pre-desert zone), such as the desert wheatear *O. deserti* which will often nest in the burrows of rodents. The white-crowned wheatear *O. leucopygia* is a true inhabitant of the desert. Basically an insectivore, it also catches small lizards, and it makes good use of the water that its prey contains.

Locusts and scorpions

There are two kinds of desert locusts: the nomadic *Nomadacris septemfasciata* and the migratory locust *Locusta migratoria* (see p. 1465). Migratory locusts can exist without drinking, though not without food. Thanks to their special bodily arrangement they are absolutely impervious to heat. They can absorb any form of vegetation whatsoever—even the most dried out—and, despite everything, extract water from it, which is an essential internal process in the desert. Furthermore, their bodies can perspire and so keep cool and they can alight quite happily on burning sand.

There are four groups of scorpions (p. 2165) living in Africa, three of which are worth mentioning. The Sahara scorpion (of the genus *Androctonus*) is deadly poisonous. The Emperor scorpion *Pandinus imperator* lives more in Central Africa and the North African scorpion *Buthus occitanus* is extremely dangerous to man. All scorpions have an organic faculty for water retention. In very dry seasons they are active at night and dig out burrows with the help of their powerful pincers.

Reptiles

Monitor lizards (p. 1641) all look alike in everything but size. The largest, the Komodo dragon (p. 1387) from that small island, grows to 10 ft long, while the smallest,

A caravan of dromedaries, the riding breed of the one-humped camel, in the Sahara.

which lives in Australia, only measures 8 in. The desert monitor *Varanus griseus*, improperly called a snake by the natives of north-west Bangladesh, can expand itself and swallow huge prey. This desert monitor lives in burrows and has an uncanny knack of finding its way home after each excursion. The Nile monitor, on the other hand, likes water and is an excellent swimmer.

The common agama lizard *Agama agama* (p. 59) is found all over Africa. The desert agama *A. mutabilis* feeds on grasshoppers and lives in the Sahara. Spiny-tailed agamas of the genus *Uromastyx*, which are lizards with a spiny tail, are also found in North Africa and are herbivorous. The common chameleon *Chamaeleo chamaeleon* (p. 546) lives at the limit of oases, chiefly in Ethiopia and Somalia, and is also found in the Nile delta. It is said to be able to tolerate great differences in temperature. The skink, or sand-fish, is also worth mentioning. There are at least 800 species of skinks throughout the world. The desert skink *Scincus scincus* gives the impression of swimming in the sand—hence its popular name of sand-fish (see p. 2272). It has been known since the most distant times and was once hunted—as it was thought to be an aphrodisiac.

The sand-snake of the genus *Psammophis* is widespread throughout the continent. The desert species are more agile than their relations in other regions. The sand-boa *Eryx* is aptly named as it has a liking for arid and sandy regions, while most other members of the colubrid snakes belong in humid areas of abundant vegetation.

Mongoose and snake

Africa is a land of cobras (p. 595). Egypt has the renowned Egyptian cobra *Naje haje*, the so-called asp (see p. 233) with which Cleopatra committed suicide. Further south there are the spitting cobras and several other true cobra species. But, staying north for the moment, we must mention the saw-scaled viper *Echis carinatus*. This 2 ft long snake has a highly toxic venom and is dangerously aggressive. It is widespread in western Asia and is found throughout the desert areas of North Africa. Two vipers live in the Sahara itself and adjacent zones. The horned viper *Cerastes cerastes*, which owes its name to the two pointed horn-like scales above its eyes, lives in areas of very sparse vegatation. The sand viper, or Avicen viper *Cerastes viper* lacks horns and is smaller; it thrives in the sands of total desert.

No mention of snakes would be complete without a word about the mongoose (p. 1638), which is famous for its deadly fights with them. The ichneumon mongoose *Herpestes ichneumon*, which is also known as Pharaoh's rat, is found in several regions and has been present in North Africa for a considerable time. The mongoose does

Eric Hosking

The banded mongoose Mungos mungo *is one of the commonest African mongooses.*

A swarm of locusts, in the process of completely defoliating a bush.

Robert – Jacana

appear to be immune to some degree to snakes' venom and is so lithe and quick that it can usually grab a snake behind its neck, hanging on until the snake is killed.

The cat and the ant

We have spoken of the desert's scarcity of water and burning sands. One would hardly expect to find a member of the cat family in this sort of region. Yet that is precisely the case with the sand cat *Felis margarita*. It is well adapted to life in this hostile environment, to the point where its paws are even provided with long protective fur which grows right up under the soles of its feet. Like so many desert creatures, it hunts at night.

At times when the temperature exceeds 50°C/120°F, normal activity is no longer possible for the majority of animals, unless they can compensate in some way (such as burrowing). All the same, life is ever present in the desert and in these burning surroundings the ant *Cataglyphis bombycina* remains active, even at temperatures above 50°C. Only three insects can achieve this—out of at least 120 species of sand-loving insects that are found in the Sahara alone.

Temperatures

Contrary to what one might think, Africa's really high temperatures do not occur in its equatorial regions, but in its tropical and sub-tropical ones—especially those that are very dry, and have few clouds. The continent thus has a thermal equator quite distinct from the geographical one. In July, this thermal equator passes almost dead centre through the Sahara.

Desiccation

On a worldwide scale, desiccation is the transformation of a relatively humid region into desert, as the climate becomes increasingly dry. In the majority of cases, it takes place over millions of years. But a contemporary example from Kenya shows how this can come about more rapidly by the actions of man. In the words of a Nairobi daily newspaper: 'Among equatorial countries, Kenya already has the appearance of a virtual desert. A desert of sand and stone spreads out just one day's journey from the centre of Nairobi.' Forests are being destroyed, and land cleared, by burning. In 1963 forests covered an area of 4265 000 000 acres. The last census of 1975 shows a *loss* of 153 000 000 acres. In 1974 alone, 2629 acres of planted trees and 32 904 acres of natural forests were destroyed by fire.

Continuing south

Leaving the desert proper through semi-desert and oases, we come to a region of pseudo-steppe. All sorts of names have been given to this type of landscape, which consists of a sort of no-man's-land that is

Desert puff adders of the genus Bitis. *Their side-winding movement leaves tell-tale signs in the sand.*

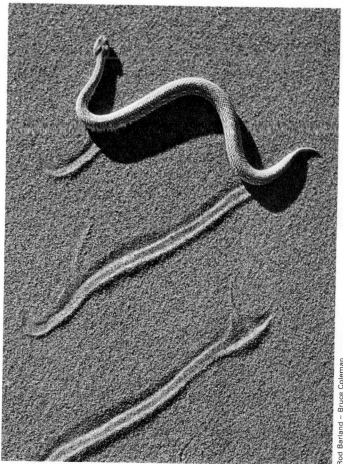

The mountainous Aïr region of the southern Sahara desert in the republic of Niger, near to Agadès.

Tanzania — the savanna countryside near Ngorongoro.

frequently encountered in Africa. We are approaching savanna, steppe and thorny bush that extend as far as the open forests of the Sudan. In terms of countries, this region comprises part of Mauritania, Mali, Nigeria, Chad, the Sudan, Ethiopia and Somalia. It is a band of territory stretching across the continent from Dakar to Djibouti, and including all the low-lying regions of Ethiopia, all of Somalia, almost the whole of Kenya and a large section of Tanzania. All these countries have a mosaic of vegetation; all have grassy savanna and open-forest savanna. A similar arrangement is found in south-west Africa and a good part of South Africa, although the south has the dry savannas of Botswana and Zimbabwe Rhodesia and there are certain differences.

It is far from easy to differentiate exactly between so-called grassy landscapes and forested ones. There are far too many transitional forms and very few plant formations exist in a pure state anyway. So definitions will be arbitrary, with some contradictions in terms—for instance, wooded steppe.

Climatic changes

The line that separates the Saharan and the Sahelian climates passes through the centre of Nigeria and bends away in the region of the 16th parallel to the north of Lake Chad. This country is dominated by the Sahelian mountains of Aïr, which extend their climatic influence a long way ahead of them. Everything of importance here takes place south of the 16th parallel. The same applies to Mali, which has three entirely distinct geographical zones: desert in the north, then a Sahelian zone of relative dryness covered with steppe—but which changes into savanna as it progresses southwards. (With the exception of certain fertilized valleys, the centre of Mali is largely marshland as a result of the flooding of numerous branches of the River Niger.) Finally, there is the third zone—the Sudanese region—which starts as savanna, and becomes wooded savanna as it goes south.

These two countries exemplify the natural limits of a vast zone—the Sahel of tropical Africa, south of the Sahara—which is transitional between desert and Sudanese climates. The word Sahel means bank and comes from the Arabic *sahil*. It designates certain developed regions of North Africa. (The Sahel is also a desert wind which blows in the south of Morocco.)

The biogeographical zones

To enable us to understand the extremely mixed character of African fauna we need to establish five biogeographic zones. The first is the *Saharan zone* which has already been dealt with; then comes the *Sahelian*, where the annual rainfall is around 12 in.—which allows a scanty growth of vegetation. In its higher regions, this zone is a little more humid, but only in the south, where 12–20 in. of rain falls during the summer, is there any cultivation.

The *Sudanese zone* comes next. Its plant life is quite different as there is rain in several months of the year. The savanna here has more trees and high grass. During the rainy season this grass can form a dense carpet and is a favoured habitat for large herbivores. In the dry season, the grass goes yellow and tinder-dry and immense regions can catch fire—which results in the notorious fires of the African bush.

The *Guinean zone* lies somewhere between what one could broadly call savanna and forest. There are a considerable number of these wooded savannas between Guinea and the Sudan. The final biogeographic zone lies further south still and consists of the dense forests of great humid regions. This group can itself be separated into the forests of Guinea and those of the Congo.

The Ethiopian region

On the worldwide scale of great zoogeographic zones the region of Africa south of the Sahara is known as the *Ethiopian region*. The north of the continent is considered as part of the Palaearctic region. Madagascar is usually included within the Ethiopian region, but, because of its unique fauna is often considered on its own. Zoogeography is based on areas of animal dispersion, and its regions are therefore characterized by the endemic groups of animals that live there. For example, endemic Ethiopian species include the hippopotamus, the giraffe and the ostrich.

The pecularities of Ethiopian fauna are chiefly due to the fact that Africa was isolated—first by continental drift and then, at a later date, by the desert barrier which effectively cut off everything south of it from the rest of the world. It is believed that the animal populations which became endemic reached this region before the deserts, particularly the Sahara, were formed. North Africa was once wholly verdant, and even zebra (p. 2782) lived there. Now, though, one needs to go to Ethiopia to find Grevy's zebra, *Equus grevyi*—to Somalia and Kenya for Grant's zebra, and Tanzania for Boehm's zebra. (Most zebras live in the eastern and southern regions of the continent.)

The North African race of ostrich, *Struthio camelus camelus* (p. 1779), is still present in West Africa. Another kind of ostrich, *Struthio camelus molybdophanes*, lives in Somalia in what is known as the horn of Africa. Other races of ostrich in northern regions have disappeared entirely.

Animal distribution

A map of Africa representing vegetation will only give an imperfect picture of animal distribution. There is, of course, a considerable connection between the two, but animals are mobile; so they cannot be easily compartmentalized. Palaearctic birds, for example, travel from Europe across the Sahara, at least as far as the southern Sahelian region. Mammals move in the opposite direction, and tend to go from the centre of Africa towards dry zones according to species and seasons.

An interesting phenomenon of bird migration is the way migratory species can leave Europe, reach tropical Africa and clearly not upset the indigenous birds that already live there. But all migration is conditioned by an impoverishment of food supplies in the region left and an abundance of food in the place the migrator visits, so there is no question of saturation. In a favourable season, migrators only consume a surplus of food which would otherwise go to waste. During a bad or dry season it is the indigen-

Boizot – Explorer

Lakeside savanna in the west of Sudan.

The shoreline of the Indian Ocean in Kenya.

Kernie – Explorer

ous birds (insofar as they are not semi-migrators themselves) that suffer a reduction of their numbers. In a good season, however, there is room for everyone.

African birds: wonderful variety

There are nearly 1500 different species of birds to be found on the African continent. Their classification according to regions would be both difficult and confusing. In Kenya alone, for instance, there are around 600 species. Only an expert can assign them all to their proper ecological niche.

There are only six species of colies (p. 1665) and these are exclusively African. Colies, or mousebirds, are parakeet-sized; highly gregarious, fruit-eating birds. It is not easy to be precise about them. They change their location very quickly according to seasons, and like many birds, the regularity of their reproductive cycle can vary under the influence of climatic circumstances.

Birds know instinctively when to choose the best moment to breed (which is when there is the most food available). But in Africa–particularly in the tropics and equatorial zones–climatic variations are not necessarily abrupt. As a result, there is a certain general stability in the behaviour of birds. With fairly constant food supplies and stable climatic conditions, birds can be found which nest at any time of the year.

African birds come in every imaginable shape, size and colour. Their appearance is astonishingly diversified and several books have been written about them alone. The colie mentioned above is an attractive arboreal bird with a distinctive small crest and a very long and rigid tail. The colies, as well as being excellent climbers, have perfected the art of moving at top speed through undergrowth. These grey mousebirds are not named solely because of their colour. As they move on the ground they shuffle along on the back of their legs, using them more like feet.

Another endemic group, the turacos, or plantain-eaters (p. 2605), numbers 18 species on the African mainland alone. Most of them live in the forest, but the grey, streaked turaco *Crinifer africanus* is most at home in the savannas and bush of West Africa. Turacos all have different habitats, according to the particular group to which they belong. There are four basic kinds of turaco. Giant turacos live in the Congo basin, do not move far, and like to roost in the tops of very thickly leaved trees. Crested turacos appear to be the shy members of the family, but as a whole its members have cautious and secretive ways. All, in general, make themselves conspicuous by virtue of their loud and resonant call.

Overall, Africa has its own very special families of birds, which are themselves abundantly diversified. It is also a land favoured by weaver-birds (p. 2692), bulbuls (p. 433),

Wilhelm Möller: Ardea

The shoebill Balaeniceps rex *is also known as the whale-headed stork.*

A herd of zebras on the run. An individual is difficult to distinguish in the midst of the group and this safeguards it against enemies.

Bruce Coleman

hornbills (p. 1236), shrikes (p. 2246), oxpeckers (p. 1793), bald crows or picthartes and very many other species.

Three special birds

Three particular species of birds are worth pointing out. The strangest of them all is the secretary bird (p. 2212). For a long time it was classed with bustards, but the secretary bird *Sagittarius serpentarius* is the only one of its species and originates from the region of the southern Sahara. It is also called serpent-eater—and for good reason. The favourite prey of this long-legged bustard-like bird is snakes.

The other two characteristic species are the shoebill, or whale-headed stork (p. 2241), and the hammerhead, which are both waders. The first lives in marshy regions, principally in the Sudan and Uganda. The hammerhead *Scopus umbretta* (p. 1146) is spread throughout all Africa south of the Sahara, wherever there is a river or low marsh water.

The shoebill lives alone or in pairs. A fairly fierce bird, it builds its nest on a platform of grasses in swamps. The hammerhead has been the subject of debate with regard to its classification, but is now classed among the order Ciconiiformes which include the ibises, herons and storks. A small bird, it is often seen perching on the backs of hippopotamuses and even crocodiles in rivers, using them as islands or observation platforms while it searches for food in the river. These birds like to live by water with trees nearby—in which they construct incredibly large, covered nests.

General considerations

Seasonal displacements or semi-migrations are another factor of animal life on the African continent. For example, the Abdim stork *Ciconia (Sphenorhynchus) abdimii* nests from Senegal to the Red Sea during the summer and winters in the southern hemisphere. The nightjar *Caprimulgus* (p. 1718), on the other hand, nests in the south in Zimbabwe Rhodesia and during the rainy season moves north into the Sudan–Sahelian zone. The behaviour of some mammals, such as the oryx and addax, is also influenced by the rains and they certainly alter their location—though it would be exaggerating to call this a migration.

The great African lakes exert an influence on the climate and vegetation around them, as of course does latitude. Forest fauna will crop up again in parallel sectors. Each time one finds a well established and typical African biogeographic zone, one will find (with a few exceptions) animals belonging to a fauna which itself is also typical. Thus the Sahelian zone repeats itself in southern Africa as soon as the desert ends, and this zone almost always inter-relates with the

The ostrich's ancestors lived in vast territories in Asia, Europe and Africa during the Eocene epoch. The African ostrich of today is the largest living bird.

fauna of the savanna. But Africa offers this peculiarity: in the east and the south there are hoofed mammals of the order Ungulata such as certain antelopes and zebras, which live nowhere else. There are no marsupials and no monotremes in Africa. The country is also quite devoid of mole species, beavers and bears, and there is only one representative deer of the family Cervidae on the continent: the sub-species of red deer (p. 2058) *Cervus elaphus barbarus*, which lives in North Africa. This is a remarkable 'relic' case that is often cited by naturalists.

Areas of distribution

Zoogeography is the study of each great region and then of sub-regions and provinces. Certain experts class the Cape as a region apart, some because of its relatively small geographical size; others on a more biological basis—as its animal populations are quite different from those of the rest of the continent. There are more endemic species there than elsewhere. The climate is also different; temperatures can reach even freezing point in the Transvaal.

In fact, looking at fauna in terms of regions can be self-defeating. The study of animal distribution involves a good deal of precision and subtlety—and, to call species truly endemic, the most minimal differences between them need to be taken into account. One way of going about it is to divide a

Hammerheads prefer to stand in shallow water and can often be seen standing on the backs of hippos.

The secretary bird. Its name derives from the black crest of feathers which resemble the quill pens that 18th-century clerks carried in their wigs.

The hadada ibis Bostrychia hagedash. *It feeds on small water animals, such as frogs and worms.*

broad zone into several natural domains and discover the species there as best one can. The notion of endemism is founded on a quantitative element. One therefore needs to take a census of animal populations. There are numerous and diverse ways of doing this and when they concern very large gatherings of populations, their accuracy is somewhat suspect. The study of a simple species is a better method. But it is virtually useless to assess the endemism of certain species on the basis of a very small territory; for example, one square mile. The rate of endemism in a territory, or the number of species one might call endemic, is calculated in percentages, in relation to all the indigenous species of the same class.

African fauna is extremely rich, and the examination of animal populations is never easy in a terrestrial community. Some forests, certainly in terms of parallel studies, are particularly inaccessible. In discovered territories, one needs to compare the inventories of territories in pairs before proceeding to evaluations, and characterize each territory in terms of the other. Deciding what fauna is of origin in a region requires considerable care.

Fish, frog and tortoise

A good number of animals are typically African, while others are frankly archaic. Fish offer several good examples. Bichirs

The white stork Ciconia ciconia *which will interrupt its migratory flight in East Africa for plentiful food when there is a plague of locusts.*

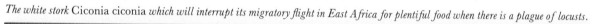

Okapia

△ *Lungfish live in stagnant water. In summer, when the water evaporates, they burrow into the mud and remain there until the rains return again.*

▷ *The peripatus is dependent on moist conditions. It is a relic from the past and links soft-bodied ringed worms with hard-bodied arthropods.*

▽ *Lions on the savanna, an Africa biome. Grass, even though it is rare, is the fundamental basis of life here. Antelopes, which feed on the grass, are themselves killed and eaten by lions.*

Morishige Mita

(p. 330) of the genus *Polypterus* are primitive fresh water creatures of which there are ten species. They are related to the lungfishes (p. 1484), and the famous coelacanth, the 'living fossil' fish living in deep waters off south-east Africa.

The goliath frog *Gigantorana goliath*, which is the largest frog in the world, is an endemic species, with a total length of about three feet and a weight of around 6½ lb.

Hinge-back tortoises of the genus *Kinixys* are excellent examples of wide distribution. Of four species, one, *K. areolatus*, lives in the Cape. The other three are interesting in the sense that two, the species *K. homeana*, and *K. erosa*, belong typically in the equatorial forest; while the other species, *K. belliana* is definitely of the savanna.

Thousands of species

The reasons why certain species of animals are found in some places and not in others is a fascinating question—and the search for an answer goes on. We know of about 4500 mammalian species in the world and millions of kinds of insects, probably more than 4 000 000. Furthermore, there remains a good deal of room for the estimation and analysis of imaginary populations. In his *Ecological Genetics*, E. B. Ford made a statement: 'It is completely unrealistic to consider the behaviour of a large interbreeding community under constant conditions since that situation, far from being realized, is not even approached in nature. The great effects of environmental stability are, moreover, reinforced by the continued repetition of qualitative and quantitative ecological changes which may be only a remote consequence of them: for an organism has not the same adaptive requirements when abundant as when rare, or when the plant and animal forms which impinge upon it are so.' Moreover, Wright remarks that: 'the environment, living and non-living, of any species is actually in continual change.' (*The roles of mutation, inbreeding, crossbreeding and selection in evolution*)

Typically African

People think of Africa in terms of lions, hippopotamuses, giraffes, rhinoceroses and monkeys. Of course its fauna is far more complex than that, but it is handy to have an image of the country which, if not entirely realistic, is at least ready made. In dealing with lesser known creatures, one needs to choose rather more carefully, though. Among fish, for instance, the tiger fish *Hydrocyon* is immensely voracious—but the species *Eugnathichthys* mainly feeds on the fins of other fish.

The African giant snail *Achatina fulica* (p. 1026) is a real agricultural bane and will eat approximately ½ oz. of leaves a day. The termite-eating aardvark *Orycteropus afer* (p. 7) in its own very special way could not be more typically African. The only representative of the mammalian order Tubulidentata, this strange creature has a tubular skull and a long prehensile tongue. For a long time naturalists have related it to the pangolins (p. 1829). But its origin is obscure, although fossils of the order date back to the Eocene in North America. The aardvark is nicknamed 'earth-pig', but it is not really very pig-like and, in fact, this native African mammal is

40

difficult to compare with any other mammalian creature.

Numerous smaller animals

Among the coelenterates, or cnidaria, a genus of hydra (p. 1283), the well studied hydrozoan of schools, is known in tropical Africa and even in the Sahara. Fresh water crustaceans are well represented and fresh water crabs, of the family Popamonidae, are widely spread. Certain shrimps are well adapted to African environments and the spiny Cape lobster, *Jasus lalendei*, is considered a delicacy. It is worth pointing out that there are no crayfish (family Asticidae) in Africa and they are only found in the northern hemisphere. However, in Madagascar, we find a family that is very close—the Parastacidae.

Apart from some northern freshwater shrimps (*Gammarus*, p. 2249), amphipods are extremely rare in Africa. One species lives subterrestrially in the Congo, and another species is found in southern Africa. There is also one fascinating case of a crustacean less than ⅛ in. long. This pancarid was discovered deep inland in an oasis in Tunisia. If the temperature of the water it lives in falls below 30°C/48°F, it dies. But it will paddle about happily in temperatures of more than 45°C/57°F. It originally no doubt came from the sea, a very long time ago, by means of underground waters. A similar discovery was made in Texas, which is considered as a sort of proof of this theory. But much still remains to be discovered about the species *Thermosbaena mirabilis*, and the five other members of its super-order.

Gondwanaland once more

Peripatus (p. 1876), which is an archaic jointed animal often termed a 'living fossil', takes us back to classification on a geographic plane. A biogeographical argument has been built around this little animal. Its present distribution seems to confirm the theory of ancient dislocation. The disclosed zoogeographic relationships (that still exist) in the southern hemisphere help one subscribe to this theory. On the subject of the southern hemisphere, it is worth remembering that Antarctica was once part of Gondwanaland. Its degree of ice only became amplified at a later date as a result of the effects of altitude and the entire ice-cap is a survival of the last ice age.

Without admitting an ancient common origin, the present areas of animal distribution—separated by oceans—would be practically inconceivable. Peripatus species are found in South America, Australia and South Africa. This in itself supports the conviction of certain naturalists that Africa south of the Sahara should be considered as a separate biogeographic region.

Scorpions and termites

Africa would be inconceivable without scorpions and termites. Scorpions date from the Silurian period, over 400 000 000 years ago, when their ancestors were perhaps still aquatic. But they became land-dwellers and have remained almost unchanged right up to the present day. Each species has its own well demarcated habitat. The scorpion *Pandinus imperator* prefers humid zones, but other scorpions tend to favour drier, even desert

Devez – Jacana

regions as we have already discussed. A detailed examination of scorpions reveals a good deal about adaptation.

Scorpions cannot exist for very long without feeding and are capable of entering into a state of lethargy. Their distribution is very unequal according to species—of which there are, all told, more than 600. They are found on all continents except Antarctica, but in each biogeographic zone they differ in species. They are most widely represented in hot parts of the world, and yet there is a species that lives in the Alps. Scorpions are arachnids and form part of the genera *Buthus*, *Euscorpius* and *Pandinus*. These last are the largest and can grow up to 8 in. long.

Scorpions are solitary creatures and if they are spotted in groups, those groups will consist only of young. Termites, on the other hand, are social animals that live in large, well-organized colonies. They belong to the order Isoptera, which is generously represented in Africa. It consists principally of termites, which are also called white ants. All told, there are 200 kinds and 2000 species of termite, not all of which are found in Africa; many species live in Australia. But one of the distinctive sights of the African savanna is its high columns of termite hills made by the soldier termites *Bellicostermes bellicosus* and, in Natal, *B. natalensis*. In the virgin forest their mounds are more mushroom-shaped. Perhaps most impressive of all are the small rounded domes constructed by the goliath termites, which are extremely wide—and up to 16 ft high.

Fish

North Africa has its own special fish as well as cosmopolitan varieties, such as sticklebacks of the family Gasterosteidae and others. North Africa apart, there are some exclusively African families and a roughly equal number which are found elsewhere. Of these, 10 originate in the sea, 15 in fresh water; and the ichthyology of African fresh water presents a mass of special features.

The 15 freshwater families all have their sources among different orders. The African polypterids are a single family, living in fresh mainland water. But this family sub-divides into two groups, with nine species in the first and only one in the second. Without going into a systematic nomenclature, we shall just say that the West African reedfish *Calamoichthys calabaricus* is of the family Polypteridae, and so is the bichir *Polypterus bichir* found in the Nile. All polypterids are distinguished by their singular dorsal fin and by the way they use their pectorals. These are fish of an ancient type. Their body is entirely covered with large glazed scales—a sort of armour—which all fish of the long distant past once had. These glazed scales are juxtaposed and those known as 'elasmoid' are laid out over the creature's skin rather like tiles.

Within the order Gonorhynchiformes are many extraordinary fish. They too are the last surviving representatives of groups that were hitherto numerous. They are all quite different from one another, but have been placed in somewhat arbitrary orders, in which there is often only one species in a

Scorpio manrus *one of many scorpion species.*

At this distance, a termite hill resembles the ruins of a building. Termites live in well-organized societies.

family. Classification varies from one authority to another. One specimen of this strange group, genus *Parakneria*, has a large flattened head and horizontal pectoral fins, which support it well in the currents of the rivers of Angola and Rhodesia. The principal families are the milkfish of the Chanidae, the Kneriidae, the Cromeriidae, the sandfish or beaked salmon of the Gonorhynchidae, the Grasseichthyidae and the Phractolemidae.

Another characteristically African fish, the pantodon or butterfly-fish *Pantodon buchholzi* (p. 471) is a West African species. This fish can manoeuvre at great speed at the surface of the water with the aid of its fan-shaped pectoral fins. This is no doubt why it was christened 'freshwater flying fish'. In fact, it cannot fly, but can leap dramatically–some yards–out of the water of the rivers of the Niger and the Congo, to which areas it is confined.

Another fascinating example is found among the mormyrids, which contain strange-looking fish. Scientists have discovered that many if not all members are capable of producing electricity. The gymnarche *Gymnarchus niloticus* (p. 1722) is most typical of the group, and can release a stunning electrical discharge; but the Ubangi mormyrid or elephant-fish *Gnathonemus petersi* is a member of the group as well, with its distinctive elongated lower lip which looks like an elephant's trunk.

The fish of the genus *Genyomyros*, which has appendages on its chin, is a little like the European barbel, though longer. Another strange species of *Gnathonemus* has a sort of proboscis, or horn, that is equal to its own length, both lips being extended into an enormous snout. The large family Citharinidae contains many species which are good to eat and supply the native peoples of their region with a high proportion of their food. These large vase-like fish can weigh as much as 35 lb. The widespread upside-down catfish of the family Mochocidae are often known as squeakers, because of the sounds produced by the dorsal and pectoral fins rotating in their sockets. The electric catfish *Malapterurus electricus* (p. 838) measures over 3 ft and weighs more than 50 lb.

Another strange group of fish are the lungfishes, whose area of distribution is now reduced to Africa, Australia and South America. These fish are almost the only ones whose evolutionary line is often quoted, for they have kept almost all their primitive features for adaptation.

Perhaps the most representative of the continent's species are the numerous cichlids of the family Cichlidae (p. 574) of the great African lakes. The most colourful is the red or jewel cichlid *Hemichromis bimaculata*, but each environment has its own proper group. Cichlids offer ground for an interesting study on account of the way they are distributed in the world. Totally absent in some biogeographic regions (Australia and the northern hemisphere) they proliferate in Africa and are widespread in Madagascar, Central and South America, and coastal rivers and lakes of India.

The fresh-water butterfly fish Pantodon buchholzi *lives in the rivers of tropical Africa. It is not related to marine butterfly fishes.*

Mammals

The origins of mammals

The first mammals appeared on the Earth around 200 000 000 years ago. In terms of organization mammals are the most advanced vertebrates. Their ancestors were the synapsid reptiles, which had already divided into several groups by the beginning of the Mezozoic era. A group known as the therapsids were the line from which today's mammals evolved. The other reptiles either became extinct or evolved in a different manner.

In southern Africa, in the stratified beds of the Karroo, scientists have found a splendid therapsid fauna that ascends from the Permian to the Triassic. Based on such discoveries, very informative comparative studies have been carried out; but these are outside the scope of this book. Present-day mammals are divided into three subclasses; the Prothotheria (monotremes or egg-layers), Methatheria (pouched mammals or marsupials) and Eutharia (placental mammals). These groups inter-relate in a complex way and are of unequal significance, but on the African continent we will only concern ourselves with placental mammals—which is the most common type throughout the world.

All classes of mammals, including marsupials, were once represented in Africa. The placental mammals, however, showed themselves to be more adaptable and better at colonizing and, it appears, supplanted the others. Monotremes survived only in Australia and marsupials are now confined to Australasia and Central and South America.

Madagascar

We shall look separately at the fauna of the large island of Madagascar (see page 1503). In fact, Madagascar effectively forms a tiny continent apart. In many ways it is related to southern India and to Australia. But its mammalian fauna goes back to the Eocene and even to the Oligocene. Furthermore, its flora and fauna, though they have a South African hallmark, are special to the point where they form new types and species. This specialization was accomplished over 40 000 000 years, and rather than a question of degeneration, concerns an evolution process of the elaboration of new types. So Madagascar can be seen as a micro-continent—and not merely a simple island.

What is distinctive about this island is related to what was said about marsupials; though in this case it applies to lemurs. In far-off times lemurs lived in Europe and North America. Today, they have found a refuge in Madagascar. The island has the world's greatest number of species to have evolved in isolation. Some lemuroids are even as tall as a man, namely the Indri.

The survival of the most primitive species is always due essentially to their geographical isolation and an absence of major carnivores; this applies to the lemuroids of Madagascar which, had they remained mainland animals, would almost certainly have been annihilated. In the case of Madagascar, some experts are convinced that land communication with the African mainland persisted up to the early Cenozoic. The Mozambique channel would not have existed and in at least some places the island would have connected with the continent. Be that as it may, Madagascar continues to pose all sorts of problems for palaeontologists, who are forced to consider opinions on animal population which deny the existence of Gondwanaland. It is reasonable to assume that some migrations could have been made on floating objects—at least in the case of small animals. But could the entire population of an island have come about in this way? It seems unlikely, but the debate continues.

Influence of the past

Climate has always been a determinant factor in the evolution and distribution of flora and fauna. There were three major climatic fluctuations in the Earth's history sufficient to provoke fundamental changes in the distribution of animals.

At the beginning of the Cenozoic era, the general planetary climate was reasonably

Gnus live in large herds, often accompanied by zebras. Hyaenas and cape hunting dogs are their main predators and young calves are particularly vulnerable.

hot and extended a long way towards the poles. In the course of the Tertiary period, however, tropical regions became hotter–and temperate and Arctic zones a good deal colder. This obviously had an effect on animals like lemurs and many others, which came to be confined to present-day tropical regions. From that point on in time, though, their traces are lost.

A small ancestor for the mammals
The ancestor of today's mammals, including man, was small–the size of a rat. Indeed, the largest mammal that existed at the time of the Jurassic was probably no larger than the size of a small cat. It must have been a timorous creature, living hidden from the enormous reptiles that dominated the period, the dinosaurs. These first mammals, like so many still in existence today, were probably largely nocturnal, only coming out at night when the great reptiles became quiescent. Then, some 70 000 000 years ago, in the Mesozoic era, the dinosaurs disappeared and the age of mammals began in earnest, as they spread across the surface of the Earth. They began the conquest of the primary continents–and what was to be an unending biological struggle.

What is a mammal?
It is not always easy to think of that small common ancestor in relation to ourselves or, say, elephants; so it is worth considering some of the things that characterize all mammals.

Mammals are warm-blooded vertebrates (homiothermic). They have the ability to keep their body temperature constant. Also, in most cases, their bodies are covered with fur or hair and all breathe air through lungs throughout their life. Their hearts have four closed chambers (auricles and ventricles). In the majority of cases they are viviparous. Monotremes lay eggs, while marsupials and placentals develop embryonically. The formers' offspring are born at an early stage of development and complete it attached to a nipple, generally in the mother's pouch.

The sub-class Eutheria, the higher mammals, which are viviparous and nourished during development by means of a placenta–forms the vast majority of present-day mammals. They are divided into numerous orders, which are defined according to dentition and eating habits–or according to the structure of limbs and occasionally their means of locomotion. Man *Homo sapiens* is regarded as the highest mammal evolved, and has his own family, the Hominidae, within the order Primates, which includes the lemurs, monkeys and apes.

Smallest and largest
Insectivores are the most primitive placental mammals, and this group contains the shrews that do not grow to much more than 2 in. long. In contrast, the largest land mammal, the elephant, is in one of the smallest orders and has only two living species–the Asian elephant *Elephas indicus* and the African *Loxodonta africana*.

The question of the relative sizes of animals introduces the notion of occupation of 'empty space' put forward by Guenot in his theory of pre-adaptation. Clearly the type and availability of food is a determinant factor. The general behaviour of individuals, which are apt to take the best ecological niches, should be considered in relation to exactly what that free space has to offer, and what it imposes on them.

The mammals of the savanna

To mention all the African and Madagascan animals in existence would require a lengthy list. Even that would not be very representative if it gave all the animals without discussing the regions where their lives unfold. The only sure way of attacking the problem would be to make, map in hand, a lengthy and scrupulous general review with all the cross-referencing necessary. As that is out of the question here, we shall look at Africa's mammals in terms of very large zones. We have already discussed the desert in the north. Now let us see what there is farther south.

The elephant shrew Petrodromus tetradactylus *is one of 18 species distributed throughout Africa. These insectivores use their long noses to probe in the forest litter for their prey.*

Honey badgers Mellivora capensis *are found in Africa and in some parts of Asia.*

Zebras graze, while giraffes browse on leaves over 15 ft from the ground.

A solitary animal of the African savanna — an adult male black rhinoceros.

The savannas of western and central Africa

Two insectivores of the tropical savannas of western and central Africa are the hedgehog (p. 1184) and the elephant-shrew *Elephantulus* (p. 851). Among the primates there are: the patas or red monkey (p. 1852), the vervet or grivet, three baboons (p. 268) the doguera, Guinean, and hamadryas—and the little galago (a bushbaby) of Senegal (p. 457).

Pangolins (p. 1829) are strange mammals which constitute an order all by themselves. There are two savanna species: the giant pangolin and the ground pangolin, which inhabits dry and sandy regions. Our list ends with three hares: the short-eared hare, which is typical of the savannas, the Cape hare *Lepus capensis* and the species *L. habessinious*.

Some rodents present in these regions are: the Gambian squirrel, the tree squirrel *Parexerus* and the ground squirrel *Xerus erythrops*, which is the only really ground-living squirrel in West Africa. The Gambian rat, which is exclusively vegetarian, lives in the arboreal savanna and forest. African cane rats *Thryonomys* (see p. 1279) look like large guineapigs but can grow to 9 in. and weigh 17 lb.

Carnivores of the savanna

A pride of lions (p. 1450) is a typical sight on the grassy plains of Africa. Each pride roams over a vast domain, for the most part consisting of open or sparsely wooded savanna (though this does not exclude mountainous and sub-desert regions). The serval (p. 2217), a large and sleek high-standing cat with big, pricked-up ears, also belongs on the open savannas. It forms a widespread brotherhood with the caracal *Felis caracal* (p. 506) and the African wild cat *F. libyca* (see p. 522). Also known as the African lynx, the caracal is found throughout the savannas, though it does not willingly enter thickly wooded forest. It is also found in the warmer parts of the Old World.

Lords of the savanna, the cheetah (p. 550) and leopard (p. 1436), hunt similar prey, usually in different places. The cheetah is a plain-dweller and the leopard more a denizen of wooded and forested terrain, so usual-

The black-backed jackal Canis mesomelas *is one of three species of jackal found in Africa. It lives in wooded and open country, scavenging and hunting small antelope.*

ly they are not in competition. Among the smaller carnivores of the civet and polecat groups, the zorilla (an African skunk relative), honey badger (p. 1218), several species of mongoose (p. 1638) and the African civet (p. 432) are worth noting.

Moving on to the dog family, the Cape hunting dog *Lycaon pictus* (p. 496) looks rather like a large dog with the head of a hyena. The bat-eared fox *Otocyon megalótis* (p. 303), which resembles a small fox with long legs, can sometimes pass for a young jackal, though it is characterized by its enormous ears. Next come the Asiatic or golden jackal *Canis aureus* and the side-striped jackal *C. adustus* (see p. 1306). Finally, it would be unthinkable in such a large area of Africa not to mention representatives of two vital families: namely, the aardwolf *Aproteles cristatus* (p. 10) and the spotted hyaena *Crocuta crocuta* (p. 1280). In fact, the aardwolf is a miniature replica of the hyaena. An insect-eater and mostly nocturnal, it is sometimes mistaken under poor sighting conditions for either a hyaena or jackal.

A spotted hyaena Crocuta crocuta *setting out to join the pack for a night's hunting.*

Other savanna-dwellers

The other mammals of the great plains include the aardvark (p. 7), the elephant (p. 842) and odd-toed ungulates (order Perissodactyla), such as Grevy's zebra (p. 2782) and the black rhinoceros (p. 2082). Even-toed ungulates (order Artiodactyla) are numerous in Africa, especially on the savanna. They include giraffe (p. 1034), gazelle (p. 1005) duiker (p. 809), gerenuk (p. 1017), dibatag (p. 767), sable antelope (p. 2123), springbok (p. 2361), great kudu (p. 1392), Derby eland (p. 835), dik-dik (p. 768), African buffalo (p. 494) and many others.

A Land of contrasts

Africa is a land of absolute contrasts. At exactly the same latitude, some 3° from the equator, there is in the east Mount Kilimanjaro with its eternal snows—and in the west, the tropical jungles of the Congo basin. The savannas of West Africa have an average altitude of 1000 to 1300 ft, the savannas of East Africa a mean altitude of 3000 ft. Again,

The eland is the heaviest of the African antelopes.

△ *Blesbok* Damaliscus albifrons *graze on the short grass of high, open ground. Early settlers recorded large herds, but their numbers have since dwindled.*

▽ *Black colobus monkeys rarely leave the trees.*

not always follow on from, or give way to, dense forests, as one might expect. Instead, the two are often separated by the sudden appearance of a poor and barren savanna. Even when regions receive the same quantity of rain and appear to have comparable soil, there can be differences between them. All of which shows how careful one needs to be in classifying geographical habitats.

The East African savanna

There is a clear difference in climate between the savannas of East and West Africa and this is due largely to altitude. The East African savannas have an average yearly rainfall of 21 in., but this increases according to how close they are to mountains. East Africa is also different in the sense that it has, to put it loosely, two rainy seasons in Tanzania, and one in Mozambique. But all this immense region is rich in savannas of different kinds and there is little dense forest.

In Tanzania, rainfall reaches 40 in. per annum. Grass grows very rapidly—and it is not surprising, therefore, that there are 23 species of even-toed ungulates (Artiodactyla) and 27 different carnivores. When the dry seasons come—and they really are dry—the antelopes move in thousands from one region to another. For not only are the East African species numerous and varied, they also have extremely large populations.

The East African primates include the thick-tailed bushbaby *Galago crassicaudatus* (p. 457), the blue monkey *Cercopithecus mitis* (see p. 1119) and the guerezas or colobus monkeys (p. 616). The thick-tailed bushbaby lives on the bushy savanna, although it is closely related to species which are denizens of dense forests. There are considerable variations between the guenons *Cercopithecus* spp), according to their particular habitats, and also between the three species of colobus monkeys.

The black-backed jackal *Canis mesomelas* (p. 1306) is found on the open savannas of East Africa—and again in the south of the continent—so the species has two quite distinct areas of dispersion. Two other carnivores, the common or small-spotted genet *Genetta genetta* and the blotched genet *Genetta*

rainfall, and the vegetation that depends on it, vary widely. In the Sahel region there is not more than 20 in. of rain each year; but go just a little further south, and the rainfall doubles and short grass and a few acacias appear. A little further south still, and one finds dry forest and very long grass around Guinea with its 60 in. of rain each year.

The lines of vegetation demarcation are, of course, not quite that simple. The boundary between dense forests and savannas can often be extremely abrupt, but it is not necessarily so. Anomalies appear in relation to regional climates and both forests and savannas can present unexpected aspects. Often, for no appreciable reason, patches of dense forest can be found right in the middle of a savanna; just as, in quite the opposite way, sizeable areas of savanna are interposed between what ought to be continuously forested zones. Again, tropical rain forest can border on all sorts of different kinds of savanna; and so-called arboreal savannas do

▽ *A Moholi or Senegal bushbaby* Galago senegalensis.

Burchell's zebra or bontequagga.

tigrina are both dry savanna-dwellers (see p. 1011): the first even goes into arid zones; while the second has a preference for the bush and does not enter thick forest. The striped hyaena (p. 1280) can also be placed in the dry savanna, although it is quite nomadic.

Two hyraxes worth pointing out in the region are the rock hyrax *Procavia capensis* and the steppe or yellow-spotted hyrax *Heterohyrax brucei* (see p. 1286). These animals form an order all on their own with 3 genera and 6–11 species (depending on the authority used). Their distribution, which is far from continuous, often results in groups of local races. But what is perhaps most interesting about hyraxes is that—even though they are only the size of a rabbit—they are considered by some zoologists to be the nearest living relative of the elephant.

Other important species in the region are Grant's zebra, Burchell's zebra (see p. 2782) and the black rhinoceros (p. 2082). It is possible that the true Burchell's zebra has entirely disappeared; but there has been so much inter-species breeding that one species comes extremely close to the ancestral stock—and so merits this name.

Artiodactyl representatives of the eastern zone include Thomson's gazelle and Grant's gazelle (p. 1005), the common eland (p. 835), the lesser kudu (p. 1392), the roan antelope and the sable antelope (p. 2123), Buffon's kob (p. 1384), Hunter's hartebeest and the brindled gnu (p. 1047).

Areas of animal distribution can overlap, of course, and in such cases species can mix together. East Africa thus has three species of jackals which can happily share the same feeding ground. Yet, if herds of Grevy's zebras and Burchell's zebras mix, as sometimes happens in Kenya, there is no question of hybridization.

Southern African savannas

In the early Permian period, southern Africa, south of the 20° latitude, was covered with ice and this influenced its entire physiography (as it did the southern part of Madagascar which was also ice-bound in the same period).

△ *Rock hyraxes* Procavia capensis *near the Cape in South Africa.*

Southern Africa is, in essence, a high plateau bordered with a narrow coastal fringe. Its base consists of crystalline rocks which were geologically folded, then shaved off; then covered with sedimentary beds which form this plateau as it is now. At its centre the plateau has an altitude of 2600–3200 ft. But its sides rise up in abrupt mountain ranges which tower over its coastlines.

More specifically, Namaland and Namaqualand form a great western plateau. The Matabele plateau stretches north. The Nieuweveld and Compassberg mountains rise in the south. In the east is Drakensberg, the most imposing formation of them all.

Southern Africa's particular physiography is worth pointing out because the country's flora and fauna are distributed as a direct result of it. The very narrow band of the southern coast has a mediterranean climate, with appropriate temperatures: 26°C/79°F at the Cape in January and 12°C/54°F in July.

▽ *Grant's gazelle is one of the largest species of gazelle.*

▽ *A herd of gnus and a few zebras at a waterhole in Tanzania.*

A female bontebok Damaliscus pygargus *and her young. Bontebok are closely related to blesbok.*

Rains are brought by cold south-west winds, and one finds palm-trees, mimosa, figs, orange-trees and vines.

Tropical climate begins in Natal, whose coastline is subjected to the influence of the warm Mozambique current. The trade wind brings good summer rains and even in winter it is not too dry. The coast is bordered with mangroves and a little way inland the country becomes savanna and forest, which border on plantations of sugar cane, coffee and tea.

The Drakensberg range, which is more than 600 miles long, stretches from the Tropic of Capricorn southwards. Exposed as it is to the trade winds, it gets a good deal of rain–80–120 in. a year, and dense equatorial-type forest grows there as a result.

The climate in the south
Overall, southern Africa has a tropical climate with a dry season. Towards the centre and west, rainfall becomes more scanty though it still coincides with very high temperatures. Furthermore, throughout the interior, temperature deviations become ac-

centuated and the dryness of the air results in very cold nights. Winds full of rain come from the Indian Ocean, discharge their loads on the first high ground they meet–and the result is that there is little water left for the lands which follow. Immediately after the Drakensberg range, the plateau of the Veld is grassy and treeless. Behind the mountains of the Cape, the Karroo is semi-desert.

The Kalahari desert, where the rainfall is only 1 in. a year, forms the low part of the enormous southern African plateau. The desert fluctuates, however, changing towards Namaland and Namaqualand into a kind of steppe. The Atlantic side of the country lies at the mercy of the cold Benguela current. This dries the region with which it connects and results in the Namib desert–which, at most, has only ½ in. of rain per year. The larger part of southern Africa's fauna, therefore, is mainly savanna type, while the Kalahari has animals comparable to those of the Sahelian zone in the north.

Southern fauna
The extent to which the resources of the

animal world have been exploited–and species have accordingly disappeared–has been exaggerated. Not all lands were suitable to support an especially rich fauna in the first place.

Even-toed ungulates are rare in southern Africa. The typical antelope of southern Africa is the springbok *Antidorcas marsupialis* (p. 2361) which lives on dry open plains. Springbok herds were once enormous. The nyala *Tragelaphus angasi* (p. 1737) is a large antelope which came very close to extinction. Apart from its introduction into parks and game reserves, this species lives in the arid regions of Botswana. The gemsbok *Oryx gazella* favours dry savanna and even semi-desert country, though it is also found in other more hospitable zones and is nomadic. The bontebok (p. 396) and blesbok (p. 376) (*Damaliscus* spp.) are quite large antelopes which have been over-hunted. The bontebok was only saved at the last moment and the blesbok is now being bred in captivity.

The mountain reedbuck *Redunca fulvorufula* (p. 2068) is an extremely graceful little antelope which lives on high hillsides. Its area of distribution is difficult to define as mountainous zones are so many in number; but what is certain is that in the south the mountain reedbuck only lives in rocky country, though not at its highest points. Another species is more numerous. This is the common reedbuck *R. arundinum*. Another species, Bohor's reedbuck *R. redunca* is found in Ethiopia. The Klipspringer (p. 1379) has a patchy distribution and, in terms of behaviour and habitat, is a sort of southern African chamois or mountain goat. The steinbok (p. 2387) belongs on open savannas or, again, in very dry regions.

Among the smaller antelopes it is worth noting the oribi and Sharp's grysbok (see p. 1767), which is a species peculiar to southern Africa. There are three southern duikers (p. 809), the Natal cephalope, the blue duiker *C. monticola* in the extreme south, and Grimm's or the grey duiker *Sylvicapra grimmia*, which is one of the few duikers to live in open country. All told there are 16 species of these small antelopes, which are widely spread throughout Africa.

In the south, the mountain zebra (p. 2782) has been saved from extinction just in time. The quagga, though, which was once a denizen of dry mountainous regions, has disappeared. A sub-species of the mountain zebra, *Equus zebra hartmannae*, lives on, but in limited numbers. These are now known as Hartmann mountain zebras—and protected. Hartmann zebras still roam free in the area where they have always lived and there are 6000–7000 of them. There is only one member of the pig family, the bush pig *Potamochoerus porcus* (p. 464) which is dark in colouring here, though in West Africa it is quite a vivid red.

Carnivores, rodents and monkeys

The south has its own species of hyaena (p. 1280), the brown hyaena. Their distribution is divided, or perhaps little known. Timid and chiefly nocturnal animals, they hide out during the day.

The caracal (p. 506) and leopard (p. 1436) are the only important southern cats. (The African wild cat is found here too, but is rare). The Cape fox *Vulpes chama* lives in dry country and is found in the Kalahari savannas and the veld. Nocturnal and extremely cautious, it remains in its earth throughout the day. It is a small canid with a silver-grey coat and can be recognized by its black-tipped bushy tail.

The black-backed jackal (p. 1306) is considered the bane of southern Africa, where it preys on poultry, and on small livestock when extremely hungry. The bat-eared fox (p. 303) is found here too, though its distribution appears to be clearly compartmentalized into eastern and southern Africa. The white-naped weasel, which looks like the European weasel, lives in open country in the south where there are few trees, though it is capable of climbing. It is a small, savage carnivore which kills a great deal more than it would need merely to feed itself.

A red lechwe stares suspiciously at the camera, ready to flee at the first hint of trouble.

Bushpigs foraging for roots. Young bushpigs can run soon after they are born.

The Cape clawless otter (p. 1786) merits classification as a savanna-dweller, for it can be found a considerable distance from the great rivers which barely cross the savanna. The slender-tailed meerkat *Suricata suricatta* (p. 1435) is a hardy little mongoose of the dry savanna; a diurnal creature, it lives in colonies.

Among the rodents, southern Africa has its own peculiar species, the Springhaas (p. 2364). It derives its name, which means 'jumping hare', from the Boers of South Africa. It is sometimes spoken of as a miniature kangaroo, but looks more like a true hare and not a rodent, such as the red hare or the Cape hare—which is poorly named as it is found from north to south along the east side of Africa.

One primate is worth mentioning: the chacma baboon, *Papio ursinus*. A tall and slender baboon, it lives in rocky environments.

Freshwater and rain forest mammals

The total surface of African lakes and rivers is 66 000 square miles (excluding marshlands).

The manatee (p. 1528) is completely adapted to aquatic existence and in fact cannot come out of the water. A large herbivorous mammal, it is found all along the Atlantic coast and also in estuaries and large rivers. In West Africa it is the species *Trichechus senegalensis* and this manatee is most numerous in Lake Chad and River

Oribis prefer to remain hidden among long grass and bushes.

A pigmy hippopotamus Choeropsis liberiensis.

Chari. The reproductive and daily aspects of sirenians are unfortunately not well known.

Equally remarkable species are the amphibious mammals, such as the otter and hippopotamus, and others which seek proximity of water without being amphibious. The reedbuck (p. 2068), for instance, is a land animal, but lives especially in zones of vegetation that are near fresh water. The waterbuck (p. 2672) likes swampy, reed-covered places and its hooves have adapted to muddy terrain, enabling it to move far and wide without any difficulty. When it gets extremely hot, this antelope will immerse itself in the water and stay there. The lechwe *Kobus leche* (p. 1425) also frequents marshes. The oribi *Ourebia ourebi* (p. 1767) which is the largest of the pygmy antelopes, is also encountered close to water. The marsh mongoose *Atilax paludinosus* (p. 1638) swims extremely well and, among other things, will devour crocodile eggs, as well as young waterfowl, fish and insects.

Turning to amphibious animals, the Cape clawless otter *Aonyx capensis* (p. 1786) is a habitual resident of slow watercourses which traverse the great rain forests; but it can also be seen on banks of sand alongside large rivers. The unmistakable hippopotamus (p. 1207) belongs to a family which only has two species: the common hippo *Hippopotamus amphibious* and the pygmy hippopotamus *Choeropsis liberensis*. The life-styles of the two are quite different and we will deal with the pygmy hippo (which is quite ferocious) when

G. Tomsich – L. Ricciarini

A hippopotamus can remain underwater for up to five minutes. As it dives, its ears and nostrils are closed. However, it often prefers to float, with only its eyes, ears and nostrils above the water.

David Hosking

A magnificent male Uganda kob, distinguished by his short lyre-shaped horns.

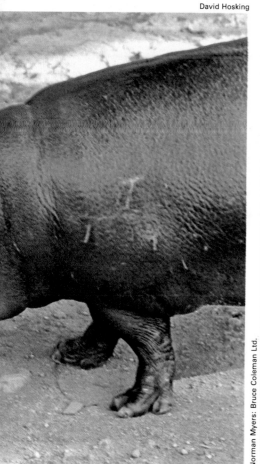

Norman Myers: Bruce Coleman Ltd.

we come to tropical forest zones. The amphibious hippo is the one usually referred to by the single word hippopotamus, without any other qualification. A sedentary creature, it remains faithful to one environment, even when there is a drought. Preferring fairly shallow water without a strong current, the hippopotamus likes to walk along river bottoms partly supported by the water. It leaves the water at night to march along regular tracks to favoured grassy places where it eats throughout the night.

The forests

Equatorial forests cover 345 000 000 acres of Africa, principally in Guinea, the Ivory Coast and the Congo. They are known as tropical rain forests. They are the characteristic feature of the equatorial zone, which has the continent's heaviest rainfall.

Mangrove forests are coastal, salt-loving forests. They grow in tropical regions on salty mud and only really thrive when they can feel the tide and where silt, consisting of brackish organic matter, is deposited. Mangrove forests have low trees and are often impenetrable. The west coast of Madagascar has belts of mangrove forest right down to the very south, while in southern Africa the mangrove limit is situated in Angola on the west coast and Mozambique on the east.

In general, a forest is defined as 'dense' or 'closed' the moment its trees take up more than two-thirds of its total surface. An 'open' forest is one where up to a quarter of its total area is occupied by trees.

Mammals of rain forests

Starting with the primates, the equatorial rain forests are the home of chimpanzees, gorillas, colobus monkeys, pottos and some monkeys of the genus *Cercopithecus* (p. 1117) to name just a few. We shall remain with the principal animals, for the equatorial forest is a region of mystery and many of the creatures that are found there are still not well known.

An elephant special to the rain forest is the sub-species, *Loxodonta africana cyclotis*. Smaller than the savanna elephant, it has rounded ears and its tusks are straight. There is also another race, *L. africana pumilio*, which is the object of some controversy, but it belongs in this particular habitat.

The genus *Gorilla* comprises one species, but there are three races, or subspecies, which inhabit different areas (see p. 1069). The mountain gorilla *Gorilla gorilla beringei* lives in the higher regions of the Congo, Ruanda and Uganda. The western gorilla *G. g. gorilla* lives on the plains of western equatorial Africa. Finally, the eastern lowland gorilla *G. g. graueri* is principally found in the lowlands of East Zaire. Wherever it may be found, however, the gorilla is a giant, the largest of the primates, and very much a resident of the last great forests which remain intact in the world.

Cercopithecus petaurista, *a white nosed monkey of the group known as guenons.*

Chimpanzees live in the tropical rain forests of Africa, where they are as much at home on the ground as they are in the trees.

A western gorilla Gorilla gorilla gorilla, *the largest of the apes.*

The okapi *Okapia johnstoni* (p. 1750) is also found in this immense region. The only living relative of the giraffe, and included in the giraffe family, it was discovered at the beginning of the century and shows how truly original the fauna of the dense tropical rain forest can be.

Chimpanzees and apes
The chimpanzee *Pan troglodytes* (p. 559) has quite an extended distribution in forest regions. It lives in dense primary forest, but not in very great numbers, and the largest chimpanzee populations occur in forests whose trees form a more open arch. (Chimpanzees also live in arboreal savannas, but that is only a secondary habitat.)

Two guenons (p. 1117) are usually given as examples of forest-dwellers: the Diana monkey *Cercopithecus diana* and the owl-faced

or Hamlyn's monkey *C. hamlyni*. But, while the Diana monkey is a true citizen of the dense forest—and particularly the high canopy, the owl-faced monkey (which is nocturnal) can be found in wooded mountainous regions.

Guenons are mainly arboreal monkeys. There are many species of guenon monkeys of the genus *Cercopithecus* and these have adapted in different ways. Various species of them are found to occupy every level of a forest. Only one ground-living species is known, the grass monkey *Cercopithecus aethips* and it is a dweller of the savanna.

Guenons that live in the same area of forest do not upset each other, each species preferring certain levels in the trees. Also, they eat different food, behave in different ways and each group occupies an ecological niche peculiar to itself.

A detailed study of guenons would be of considerable interest, both ecologically and morphologically and from the point of view of adaptation; but unfortunately there is insufficient space for it here. We should merely note that, no matter what the type of African forest, it has its guenon monkey. De Brazza's monkey *C. neglectus* is a creature of marshy forests and riversides. Allen's monkey *Allenopithecus nigrovirdis* and the talapoin *C. (Miopithecus) talapoin* also live in swampy forests. The talapoin especially favours low regions and mangrove forests in central West Africa.

The red-tailed monkey *C. ascanius*, the moustached monkey *C. cephus* and white-nosed monkey *C. nictians* all live in gallery forests. L'hoest's monkey *C. hoesti* exists in mountain forests. The mona monkey *C. mona*, which has a number of variations

The strange okapi has changed little over the last two million years.

African elephants, the largest of the two species, on the move.

between species, occupies the best positions in the middle and lower strata of dense forests.

Other primates are the black and white colobus, *Colobus polykomos* and its relation, the green colobus *Colobus verus*, which especially likes thickets in the middle of dense forests; the guereza colobus, with several sub-species; the black colobus *Colobus satanas* and the red colobus *C. badius* of West Africa, all of which are entirely typical of dense forests. Authorities vary regarding the number of species and forms (see p. 616).

The potto *Perodictus potto* (p. 1975) and the angwantibo *Arctocebus calabarensis* (p. 135) are two nocturnal and truly arboreal animals of the region. Two bushbabies (p. 457), Allen's bushbaby *Galago alleni* and the needle-clawed bushbaby *Euticus elegantulus* also live in deep forest. Demidoff's bushbaby *G. demidovii* dwells in the upper strata of dense forests, but is also represented in mountain forests. Incidentally, bushbabies are far more active and lively than pottos.

Pangolins and flying squirrels

The unique order, the *Pholidota*, has two members that live in equatorial forests: the tree pangolin *Manis triscupis* and the long-tailed tree pangolin *M. longicaudata* (see p. 1829). These strange, semi-arboreal mammals roll up into tight balls as a means of defence. The long-tailed species is well adapted to life in flooded forests—and is exceptionally arboreal, as well as being an excellent swimmer.

There are some unusual rodents here too—namely the African flying squirrels of the family Anomaluridae (p. 2159). A controversial group, they very slightly resemble the squirrels of South-East Asia and North America in appearance; but that is where all comparison ends and the African flying squirrels, called scaly-tails, need to be considered entirely apart. For a start, they are true dense forest-dwellers. Pel's scaly-tail *Anomalurus peli* with its black fur, and Jackson's scaly-tail *A. jacksoni* are typical of the rain forest, as is their relation Beecroft's scaly-tail *A. beecrofti*. The red scaly-tail lives in Gabon, the red-back in the great forests of the Cameroons and Congo. There too one encounters the dwarf scaly-tail *A. pusillus* and the pygmy scaly-tails of the genus *Idiurus*—which are true scaly-tails in miniature. Only one member of this family—the flightless scaly-tail *Zenkerella insignis*—does not have flight membranes, although it too lives in the forest.

The dense forest has its carnivores also. Among them are: the paradine genet *Genetta paradina*, the servaline genet *C. servalina*, the Victoria genet or giant genet *G. victoriae* and the very rare Villiers genet (see p. 1011). The leopard *Panthera pardus* (p. 1436) can be found in all forest habitats right up to the high zones. The golden cat *Felis aurata* ranges from the open reaches of the savanna to the confines of closed forests.

△ *A long-tailed pangolin of the African rain forests. A pangolin has no teeth; its food is ground up inside its specialized stomach.*

Janon – Jacana

An African scaly-tail uses its long claws to help it cling to the branches of trees.

Janon – Jacana

Even-toed ungulates

We have already mentioned the okapi, but there are other important forest even-toed ungulates or artiodactyles. The bongo *Taurotragus euryceros* (p. 1392), for example, lives almost exclusively in thick undergrowth and dense forest. It has at least two major species: the western bongo found at Katanga in Sierra Leone and an eastern one around Kenya. The western species lives in covered relic forests; the eastern more usually in rain forests.

Duikers, (p. 809), small antelopes whose habits are not well known, are in general divided into two large groups: forest duikers of the genus *Cephalophus*, which have relatively short legs and an arched back; and the bush duiker of the genus *Sylvicapra*, with short backs and longer legs. All told, there are 14 species and almost 45 sub-species of duikers. Some species–Jentink's duiker *C. jentinki* of the Ivory Coast, for example–occupy a very confined area. The yellow-backed or giant duiker *C. sylvicultor* is most representative of those living in the great primary forest. The black duiker, *C. niger*, Peter's duiker *C. callipygus*, the bay duiker *C. dorsalis* and Maxwell's duiker *C. maxwelli* are all dense forest creatures. The blue duiker *C. monticola*, which is the smallest of them all, lives in the most densely wooded regions. The black-fronted species, *C. nigrifons*, lives in swampy forest. Harvey's duiker *C. harveyi* lives in watery surroundings. The others of the family either live in secondary forest, mountain regions, or–in the case of the Natal duiker–dense bush. Two antelopes, Bates' dwarf antelope *Neotragus batesi* and the royal antelope *N. pygmaeus* are also worth mentioning here. They are small, like duikers, and are also dwellers of dense tropical forest, although they are not closely related. (see p. 2428).

Pygmy hippopotamuses *Choeropsis liberiensis* (p. 1207) live in pairs or alone, in marshy forests–or near rivers surrounded by dense forest. The bushpig *Potomochoerus porcus* (p. 464) is a true wild pig. It inhabits mainly the thick undergrowth of dense forests but is also found in mountain forests. Herds of bushpig which can easily number up to 30 individuals–move around a great deal in their search for food and cover a vast territory. Their coats vary with age, and also according to region: and this differentiates their various races. In southern or eastern zones, bushpigs are almost black. In West Africa they are red. The giant forest hog *Hylochoerus meinertzhageni* (p. 1023)–another heavier member of the pig family–lives in family units or small groups, and is not very sociable. It is basically a dense forest creature of the moist rain forests but, according to regions, can go out to feed on the plains. It is the largest living pig in the world.

Buffalo

African buffalo (p. 494) comprise two types of animal which differ widely in terms of size

Bruce Coleman Ltd.

△ *Duikers are the smallest and most primitive of the African antelopes. They are abundant, largely because their short horns have never been sought after as trophies.*

Tokumitsu Iwago

A leopard at a waterhole. The colouring and the arrangement of spots varies according to race.

Kakamega rain forest — one of the few remaining parts of the only rain forest in Kenya. Much rain forest has been cut down to make room for more agricultural land.

and habitat. They are a subject of controversy in that some naturalists consider them to be all one species, while others do not. At one extreme there is the great buffalo *Syncerus caffer*; at the other the little inhabitant of the forest, the red, or dwarf buffalo *S. caffer manus*. (Of course, there are intermediary forms.) We shall not examine all the circumstances that have resulted in this state of affairs, but it is worth pointing out that, in general, forest-dwellers are the smallest animals of a species; while the largest are those of the savannas. In general, however, most authorities accept that there is one uniquely African species of buffalo, which has three sub-species: the cafrerie buffalo *S. c. caffer*, the savanna buffalo *S. c. bradyceros* and the dwarf buffalo *S. c. manus*. The latter has a thick red-brown hide, fringed with yellow fur and is 3–4 ft in height at the shoulder. Its pointed horns curve backwards from its forehead, and it can move rapidly and with ease in thick forest.

Where the rain forests are found

Tropical rain forest grows in three principal regions of the world: in the Amazon, Asia and West and Central Africa–spilling over in each case into other nearby regions. On the African continent, this extension carries over to Madagascar

Africa's dense forests come to a halt some degrees from the equator. This omits the lower part of Zaire and includes Liberia, south of the Ivory Coast and a large slice of the meridional parts of Togo, Dahomey and Nigeria. A similar belt of rain forest crops up in the region of the lower Niger and the great Congolese basin, and again on the west coast of Madagascar.

Tropophile forests are also worth mentioning. These are tropical deciduous forests whose great trees lose their leaves during the dry season–though some varieties in the lower strata remain evergreen.

In all regions of really luxuriant forest, rainfall is spread throughout the year; there are no disturbing seasonal rhythms or cycles, and vegetation grows almost continuously in such favourable conditions. Animal species are very diverse; there is a multiplicity of available habitats, and an astounding abundance of food allows creatures to live without rivalry. From the top to the bottom of these forests, there is incessant life, particularly at night. Small ground animals of various groups and orders inhabit the rotting vegetation that covers the forest floor. Immediately above them live every imaginable species of butterfly and other insects as well as birds which, poor fliers though the majority may be, are very beautiful.

The cape buffalo is reputed to be the most dangerous animal in Africa, but in fact is only aggressive if approached suddenly and made to panic.

Agama

A genus of about 50 lizards belonging to the family Agamidae, which is related to the iguanas and includes in its 300 species such types as the Australian moloch or thorny devil, the frilled lizard and the flying dragons. The best known agama is the foot-long common agama of Africa, Agama agama. The male agama's head is bright terracotta, the colour of the African earth; his body and legs are dark blue; his tail banded pale blue, white, orange and black. His skin is rough to the touch, like sandpaper, and he has a dewlap of loose skin under his chin and a row of small spines on his neck like the comb of a young cock.

Other members of the genus include the starred agama (A. stellio) of the eastern Mediterranean region, and the desert agama (A. mutabilis) of North Africa. Among other genera of agamids not separately treated in this work are: Phrynocephalus (about 40 species, the toad-headed agamids), Calotes (about 25 species), Uromastix (spiny-tailed lizards), Hydrosaurus (water lizard).

Jane Burton: Photo Res.

Green crested lizard (Calotes cristatellus) *of south-east Asia, one of the Agamid family.*

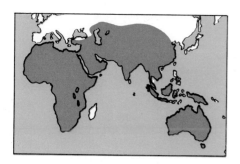

African distribution and habits

Agamas are the commonest reptiles in West Africa. Anyone who sets foot there cannot fail to notice them within the first few minutes. They are seen wherever the forest and bush have been cleared. In villages they run up and down hut walls, scamper across compounds and clatter over corrugated iron roofs, while in the main streets of the big towns thronged with people and traffic, they sunbathe in decorative groups on walls of modern stores or on ruins of houses—an urban rabble in their rubble slums.

At first sight there seems to be a confusing variety of other lizards as well. They can be seen in all sizes from five inches to a foot—some sandy, some chocolate, some with green-spotted heads, some with orange blotches on their sides. But it soon becomes clear that they are all the same species, the smallest being hatchlings, the middle-sizes females, and the largest of all, males. Only mature males that are dominant—that is, strong enough to boss other males—maintain the bright orange-and-blue colouring. Weak or subordinate males, or any that have had a bad fright, are dull brown. The mature male agama with his red face and ferocious mien looks extraordinarily like the traditional picture of a peppery colonel about to explode in an apoplectic fit.

The common agama has adapted its ways to become a companion of man, living in the thatch of huts, emerging to feed on scraps and insects, but always ready to race back to shelter if disturbed. If caught in the open it is able to run on its hind legs.

During the day the lizards are extremely active, hurtling across open spaces from one heap of stones to another, darting out to snap up ants, even leaping into the air after flying insects. Only in the afternoon, when the temperature reaches around 38°C/100°F in the shade, do they try to find a cool spot in which to lie down. As soon as it becomes a little cooler they begin to chase about again.

Towards dusk the agamas congregate in communal roosts, often in the eaves of houses, and at night all the males go a dull brown colour all over, like the subordinate males. But the next morning, when out in the early sun, their brilliant colours return.

The desert agama lives in the dry areas of North Africa, avoiding bare sand. After the cold night an agama will be literally stiff with cold, but with the sunrise it absorbs energy and its temperature rises so that it can start hunting, courting and so on. As the sun's power increases the desert agama must be careful not to overheat—although it can tolerate greater temperatures than most reptiles. The sparse scrub of the desert gives sufficient shelter to the agamas, who dash from one bush to another as they go about their daily business.

Insectivorous feeders

Agamas are mainly insectivorous, chasing their prey at speed and catching small insects with the tongue or snapping up larger ones directly with the mouth. The incisor-like front teeth are pointed like those of insectivorous mammals. Agamas may also eat grass, berries, seeds and the eggs of smaller lizards.

Polygamous breeder

The common agama is polygamous. The brilliantly coloured male may be seen with half a dozen or more females, in a territory which he defends vigorously.

In courtship the male comes alongside the female, bobbing his head, and then, if she allows him, grips her neck with his jaws. If she is out of breeding condition and does not allow this, he will continue bobbing until exhausted. If he is successful, he puts one hind leg over her back, grasps her hind leg with his foot, and twists the hind end of his body under her. The female then raises her tail away from the male and the vents are brought together.

Sometimes the female initiates the courtship by running up to the male and raising her tail in front of him. He then chases her until she lets him catch up.

Even common agamas living near the Equator have a very definite breeding season, which occurs after the 'long rains' of March-May. The males have ripe spermatozoa all the year, but the females can only lay eggs from June to September, some months after the rains. At this time the

Jane Burton: Photo Res.

△ *A male African common agama, bobbing his head in boundary threat display. The bright red head is a sign of his aggressiveness.*

▽ Agama bibroni *grows to about 10 in. from nose to tip of tail. Here the dull brownish colour suggests it is of inferior rank.*

Popperfoto

vegetation becomes lush and the insect population rises, providing the female agamas with an ample supply of protein for the formation of eggs, which are then laid in clutches of up to twelve.

The peppery colonel

The reference to peppery colonels is not without point, for agamas have their little empires to defend. In rural districts they are well spaced out, each male owning his country estate. By watching the different males it is easy to pick out each one's stronghold: a tree, a log or a rock near the middle of his territory. You can then draw fairly accurate lines marking the boundaries of these territories, and along these lines the owners battle to maintain or extend their properties.

In the towns, where agamas are thicker on the ground, the territorial instinct can lead to more frequent fighting and to situations which appear to us somewhat comic.

An illustration of this is an actual situation observed in Akure in West Africa. Close to a bungalow lived a fine male agama, readily recognisable because he had a clubbed tail, having lost an inch of tip. He was nicknamed Old Apoplexy—Apo for short—by an English family occupying the bungalow. His territory included a strip of grass with four trees and a hedge to one side. He basked much of his time beside his three 'wives', but was often engaged in fights with a neighbouring agama, 'Rival', who had five wives.

Rival had to patrol the other boundaries of his territory, and while he was absent Apo would rush in and grab one of his females, beating a speedy retreat when Rival returned. One day he failed to make a quick enough getaway. Rival drove him up a tree, higher and higher, until he lost sight of Apo, who faded to a dull grey as his fighting spirit ebbed. But Rival, after descending the tree, waited at the base for Apo.

By the following day a third male had taken over Apo's territory, and two mornings later he was still in possession. In the afternoon a club-tailed male agama, chocolate in colour, entered this territory. It was Apo, who had at last escaped. Suddenly there was a muddle of flailing feet and tails. The third lizard, caught off balance, retreated as fast as he could. Gradually, Apo, back victorious on his own territory and lord once more of three wives, changed from chocolate to grey flecked with green, and his head resumed its orange tint.

class	**Reptilia**
order	**Squamata**
suborder	**Sauria**
family	**Agamidae**
genera	*Agama* and others

60

Agouti

A genus of Central and South American rodents resembling large, long-legged guinea pigs. The numerous species vary in colour from tawny to blackish-brown with lighter underparts. Some forms have white stripes. The coarse hair is longer on the hind quarters, where it is usually bright orange or golden but may be white or black. This hair is raised when the animal is alarmed or aggressive. The head is rather rat-like, with relatively large, pinkish ears. The agouti is about 20 in. long, with a short, hairless tail and long legs. It has five toes on the fore feet and three on the hind feet; all have hooflike claws.

A close relative of the agouti is the acouchi of north-western South America (Myoprocta pratti). *The principal difference is that the acouchi has a slender, white-tipped tail which is used as a signal in courting ceremonies.*

Zool. Soc. London

△ *Agoutis are delicate eaters, sitting back on their haunches and holding their food in the fore feet, sometimes even peeling it.*

▽ *Hunted agoutis will make for water when hard pressed. They are good swimmers but cannot dive.*

South American distribution

Agoutis are abundant in forest and wooded areas throughout Central and South America from Mexico southwards to Brazil and Peru: one species is found in the Antilles. Where they are undisturbed agoutis are said to be diurnal; but they are mostly known as nocturnal animals that spend the day in holes in trees or in burrows scraped in the ground among soft limestone boulders or under the roots of trees.

The burrows are shallow 'foxholes', 2–3 ft deep, sometimes roofed over by a lattice of twigs covered with leaves. Each burrow is occupied by one animal or a small group probably consisting of a family. Well-worn tracks radiate from the entrance to the communal feeding ground.

Reports differ as to whether agoutis are social or solitary in their way of life; different species may well have different habits. It seems that, although they sleep in their burrows alone or in small groups, they gather in groups of up to 100 to feed. It is also said that they are very shy and 'highly strung'—fighting fiercely among themselves yet fleeing in panic at the first alarm,

Okapia

61

Three-toed runner

The agouti, unlike its relatives such as the guinea pig, is adapted for fast running. This drawing of an orange rumped agouti shows its long legs and the three toes on the hind feet which give minimum contact with the ground and maximum leverage.

Barry Driscoll

even jumping over cliffs *en masse*.

Despite these conflicting characteristics—fighting and fleeing—agoutis are easily tamed and make affectionate pets. They can live up to 20 years, but the average length of life is six years.

Feeding

Like all rodents agoutis are mainly vegetarians, browsing on leaves, fallen fruit and roots. Sometimes they climb trees to take green fruit. They are delicate eaters, sitting back on their haunches and holding their food in the fore feet and, if it has a tough skin, peeling it carefully with their teeth before eating it. They hoard food in small stores buried near landmarks.

Occasionally they eat the eggs of ground-nesting birds, and have even been seen searching for shellfish on the seashore.

Breeding

Litters number from two to six; in the wild two is the most common, in zoos, one. Some species have two litters each year, in May and October; others appear to breed all the year round. The young are born in a burrow lined with leaves, roots and hair. Their arrival is unusual in that the mother gives birth while in a squatting position. They are quite well developed at birth: they are covered with hair, their eyes are

open, and within an hour they are nibbling at vegetation. This advanced stage of development is linked with the long gestation period of three months.

While the young are very small the father is barred from the nest. They remain with the parents for some weeks.

Enemies

On being disturbed the agouti first freezes to avoid being detected (the young have this ability from birth): it sits with body upright and ankles flat on the ground ready to leap off at full speed. This it then does, screaming shrilly and dodging obstacles with remarkable agility.

Agoutis have been described as the 'basic diet of South American carnivores' such as the ocelot and the jaguar. Man also finds in agoutis a plentiful source of food, and they are hunted too in areas where they are pests of sugar cane and banana plantations.

One neat hunter's trick is to toss stones into the air. These, falling through the leaves and hitting the ground, sound to the agoutis like falling fruit, and so they come out to feed. Another hunting method depends on the agoutis' habit of making for water when hard pressed. They are good swimmers but cannot dive. So beaters drive the agoutis towards a river, where they are easy targets for hunters lying in wait.

Adapted for running

Agoutis are fast runners, escaping predators by speed rather than by hiding in burrows. They are very agile and bound through undergrowth undaunted by precipices, on which they display the agility of goats. Leaps of 20 ft from a standing start have been recorded.

This is surprising behaviour for an animal related to such pedestrian creatures as guinea pigs and porcupines. The reason lies in the anatomical features that distinguish the agouti from its relatives, namely its long, thin legs and the hoof-like claws on which it walks and gallops—so resembling the ungulates or hoofed mammals. The latter have become adapted for running by the development of long legs, the reduction in the number of toes and the formation of hooves—the number of toes being reduced by the animal's feet being raised so that fewer toes touch the ground. There has been a similar trend in the agoutis.

class	**Mammalia**
order	**Rodentia**
family	**Dasyproctidae**
genus	***Dasyprocta***

Alaska blackfish

A fish that lives in freshwater pools, streams and marshes in north-western Alaska, on a few islands in the Bering Straits in northern Canada and in Siberia. It is seldom found far inland, but where it does occur it is abundant and serves as food for the Eskimo and his dog. One observer has told of seeing the water courses leading from lagoons almost blocked with blackfish. The fish itself is unpretentious. It is sombrely coloured— greyish with irregular black bars—and reaches a maximum length of about 8 in. It is chubby and somewhat pike-like with its jutting lower jaw; some scientists maintain that it is related to pikes.

The Alaska blackfish has for many years been the subject of controversy as to its apparent ability to survive in blocks of ice.

△ *The Alaska blackfish is about 8 in. long. The large gills, protected by gill covers, help it to survive in adverse conditions.*

▽ *A weed-choked pond in a sphagnum bog, like those in which the blackfish makes its summer home.*

Sluggish freshwater dweller

In winter the Alaska blackfish lives in deep water, perhaps as deep as 20 ft, and moves back into depths of a few inches in the spring. In the summer it lives among dense growths of water plants and never enters clear water. It is not an active fish, although it can move at lightning speed when alarmed —reminiscent of a frog leaping from a hand put out to grasp it, or of the lightning dash of a pike.

The blackfish seems to be specialised for surviving adverse conditions. In winter it lives below the ice at temperatures approaching 0°C/32°F, while in summer the water reaches about 20°C/68°F. It is also tolerant of overcrowding to a far greater degree than most other fishes: it can stand up to competition with other species as well, both in the matter of living space and food; and it can exist in water with low oxygen content. It is perhaps this hardiness which gave rise to some of the less credible tales of survival in extreme conditions.

Food

It was once thought that the Alaska blackfish lived on plants and worms. Later studies show that it does eat both these to a slight extent, as well as small crustaceans known as water fleas; its main food, however, is insect larvae, especially those of the two-winged flies such as midges and mosquitoes.

Breeding

The blackfish spawns in June and July, and in May and June the males develop a reddish margin to the fins. There seems to be no elaborate courtship or parental care of the eggs. The fry grow quickly and the young fishes are chestnut-brown with white bellies and dark brown bars on the flanks.

The old, old, story

There is an old myth that certain animals, including the Alaska blackfish, can be frozen alive in a block of ice and revive when the ice is melted. As regards the blackfish, the myth seems to have started with a statement in Sir John Franklin's book, *First Overland Journey to Polar Seas,* about carp completely frozen being thawed before a fire and 're-covering their animation' This was in 1824; in 1882 Nordenskjöld, in his *Voyage of the Vega,* reported fishes living in a lagoon that froze to the bottom. He later modified this to 'apparently freezes' to the bottom. Four years later L. M. Turner, who explored Alaska, spoke of fish frozen in grass baskets for weeks being brought into the house, thawed out and found to be as lively as ever. He also told the story of a frozen fish thrown to one of the Eskimo dogs being swallowed and vomited up after a short while, when it was found to have been revived by the warmth of the dog's stomach.

Most laymen and many scientists swallowed these stories. But there were sceptics also, and before many years had passed investigators were using the newly invented cold stores to test them. The Russian, Borodin, was the first to be disillusioned, as the result of extensive tests carried out prior to 1934. Since then the American Scholander and his associates have found they were unable to freeze blackfish and have them survive. Another American, Walters, put some blackfish into a small pond in Alaska which he knew would freeze solid in winter. The fish did not survive.

The truth is that the story of the black-fish, including that of the one vomited by the Eskimo dog—which few writers on the fish have failed to repeat—are founded on Eskimo folk lore. Yet it is because the stories are so near to being possible that they have been so hard to refute. Goldfish, carp, tench and other species—and the blackfish —can be supercooled and still survive— under certain conditions. They can be subjected to temperatures below freezing point and, provided no ice crystals come in contact with the body, they can be resuscitated. Borodin found that the blackfish, for example, can survive 30—35 minutes exposure to −20°C/−36°F but that an hour's exposure is fatal. It should be emphasised, however, that such exposure must be in super-cooled dry air where no ice crystals can form. In other experiments it has been shown that freezing—in the true sense—even a part of the body of a blackfish results in necrosis—that is, the affected tissues are damaged beyond repair.

class	**Osteichthyes**
order	**Salmoniformes**
family	**Umbridae**
genus & species	***Dallia pectoralis***

Albatross

A family of birds in the petrel order. They are the largest members of the order and among the largest of flying birds. They have goose-sized bodies with very long, slender wings: of the 13 species, the largest is the wandering albatross, which has a wingspan sometimes exceeding 11 ft. The plumage is black and white or, in a few species, brown. In only some of the species is it possible to tell the sexes apart.

1. *Yellow-nosed albatross (Diomedea chlororhyncha) landing, showing its large wingspan. This enables it to soar for hours in the oceanic air currents.*
2. *The albatross nests on cliff tops where it can easily take off. The chick is guarded by its parents for several weeks.*
3. *Later the chick is left by itself while the parents find food for it.*
4. *Black-browed albatross (Diomedea melanophris) ranges over the oceans between 30° and 60° latitude south, breeding on such islands as Tristan da Cunha, South Georgia, and the Kerguelen and Auckland Islands. It has been recorded as a vagrant to the British Isles and even to the Arctic.*

Popperfoto

R.Burton

V.Serventy: Photo Res.

Barnaby's

Ocean wanderers

Nine species of albatross are confined to the Southern Hemisphere, breeding mainly on the sub-Antarctic and oceanic islands. Another three are found in the North Pacific, with the waved albatross on the equatorial Galapagos Islands. None breed in the North Atlantic, although fossil remains have been found in England and a few have been recorded as vagrants in modern times. These vagrants include wandering, black-browed, yellow-nosed, grey-headed, and light-mantled sooty albatrosses. One black-browed albatross appeared in a Faroese gannet colony in 1860 and for 30 years—until it was shot—it accompanied the gannets on their annual migrations. Another visited the Bass Rock gannet colony off the Scottish coast in 1967 and 1968.

The doldrums, the windless belt around the Equator, are possibly one of the reasons why so few albatrosses have been recorded in the North Atlantic, as albatrosses need a sustained wind for flight. They are heavy birds with comparatively small wing muscles, but they can remain airborne for long periods and cover vast distances because of the difference in the speed of the wind at the water's surface and some 50 ft above, due to friction slowing down the air at the surface. The albatross glides swiftly downwind and surfacewards, gathering speed. When just above the water it swings sharply round into the wind and soars up. As it rises it loses momentum and its ground speed (i.e. in relation to the water surface) decreases. Its air speed, however, does not decrease so fast, as the bird is rising and so continually meeting faster wind currents. By the time the air speed has dropped completely the albatross will have gained sufficient height to start the downward glide again.

The main haunt of albatrosses is the sub-Antarctic zone where the Roaring Forties and Howling Fifties sweep around the world and there is nearly always enough wind to keep the albatrosses aloft—although they can glide in quite gentle breezes. To increase speed the albatross 'close hauls', partly closing its wings to reduce air resistance without seriously affecting lift.

With their great wingspan and weak wing muscles albatrosses have difficulty in taking off. When there is enough wind—especially if there are thermal currents or eddies—takeoff is easy; but on still days they have to taxi, running along and flapping their wings until they have gained sufficient air speed to take off, or drop over the cliff face and glide away.

Some species are fairly confined in their range, like Buller's albatross in New Zealand; others, like the wandering, black-browed and sooty albatrosses circle the world from Tropics to Antarctic.

Marine feeders

All species of albatross feed on marine organisms living at the surface of the sea, such as fish, squid and crustaceans. They also take small sea birds on occasions, and they like refuse from ships, flopping down into the water as soon as a bucketful is tipped overboard. Sailors who have fallen overboard have reputedly been viciously attacked by albatrosses.

Cliff top breeding sites

Breeding grounds, where albatrosses gather in tens of thousands, are usually on the top of cliffs where the birds can take off easily. They are extremely faithful to their nest sites, and populations have survived such calamities as volcanic eruptions or pillage by man because the immature birds that were absent at the time later returned to breed.

Albatrosses are very long-lived birds: one recaptured 19 years after being ringed as an adult must have been at least 26 years old and wandering albatrosses may live for 70 years. They do not start breeding until at least seven years old, but young birds return to the breeding ground before then and court halfheartedly. Courtship displays of wandering albatrosses, which are to be seen throughout the breeding season, are most spectacular. The two birds of a pair dance grotesquely and awkwardly with outstretched wings, trumpeting and snapping.

A single egg is laid in a cup-shaped nest of mud and plants and is incubated by both parents for periods ranging from 65 days in the smaller species to 81 days in the larger ones. The chick is also brooded for a short time and is guarded by the adults for several weeks. It is then left by itself and both parents can be away feeding at once. They return at intervals to give the chick a huge meal of regurgitated squid, crustaceans or fish. The young of the smaller albatrosses fledge in two to three months, but larger ones may spend eight or nine months in the colony, sitting out the severe southern winter until the following summer. The parents feed them the whole time, so by the time that the young become independent it is too late for the parents to nest again and breeding is only possible in alternate years.

The young albatrosses leave the breeding grounds to glide away around the oceans. Before they return to court several years later they may circle the globe many times.

No natural enemies

Albatrosses have no natural enemies, living as they do on remote islands, except for some eggs and young being taken by skuas and giant petrels. Any introduced carnivores would, however, wreak havoc among the densely parked nests, for the sitting albatross's reaction to disturbance is just to sit tight on the nest and clack its bill. It also spits oil from digested crustaceans and fish—but this is no discouragement for determined predators.

The sailors' curse

Albatrosses have been known to sailors since the days of Magellan. Their inexpressive, fixed facial expression as they glide alongside a ship for miles on end without a flicker of the eye has brought them various nicknames: Mollymawk (from the Dutch Mallemok, 'stupid gull'), Gooney (English/American for a stupid person), Bakadori (Japanese for 'fool-birds').

But they not only had a reputation for idiocy; they were considered to be harbingers of wind and storms—not, perhaps, surprising in view of their difficulty in remaining aloft in calm weather. They were

△ *The albatross glides swiftly downwind and surfacewards, gathering speed. When just above the water it swings sharply round into the wind and soars up.*
▽ *The albatross's great wingspan is supported by relatively small muscles as it rarely flaps its wings. It remains airborne for long periods, gliding vast distances using the updraught above wave crests.*

also regarded as the reincarnations of seamen washed overboard, and it was thought extremely unlucky to kill them, as Coleridge expressed in his *Ancient Mariner*:

And I had done an hellish thing
And it would work 'em woe:
For all averr'd, I had kill'd the Bird
That made the Breeze to blow.

But, despite the chance of having an albatross hung round one's neck and suffering the far worse experience that later befell the Ancient Mariner, sailors have not always treated albatrosses kindly. Their capture on baited hooks trailed from the stern of a ship often relieved the monotony of life and diet.

More seriously, albatrosses were once favourite material for the 19th-century millinery trade, the wings sometimes being cut off the still-living birds. The North Pacific colonies bore the brunt of this fashion for plumage which, luckily, ceased before all the birds were dead.

Since the Second World War there has been another crisis for the albatross. Long-range aircraft flights have made oceanic islands necessary as staging posts, and one such is Midway Island, the home of the Laysan albatross. Not only are albatrosses using the United States Navy's runways for taking off, they also soar in the thermals above them, providing a serious danger to aircraft. Of the many methods that have been tried to reduce this danger, the most effective has been the bulldozing of dunes by the runways which cause the updraughts that the albatrosses need for flying.

class	**Aves**
order	**Procellariiformes**
family	**Diomedeidae**
genera	***Diomedea spp.*** ***Phoebetria spp.***

When annoyed, alligators open their vast jaws and roar. Male alligators also roar during their quarrels in the breeding season and to attract females.

Alligator

Two species of reptiles which, with the caimans, belong to a family closely related to the crocodiles. Alligators and crocodiles look extremely alike: the main distinguishing feature is the teeth. In a crocodile the teeth in the upper and lower jaws are in line, but in the alligator, when its mouth is shut, the upper teeth lie outside the lower. In both animals the fourth lower tooth on each side is perceptibly larger than the rest: in the crocodile this tooth fits into a notch in the upper jaw and is visible when the mouth is closed, whereas in the alligator, with the lower teeth inside the upper, it fits into a pit in the upper jaw and is lost to sight when the mouth is shut. In addition, the alligator's head is broader and shorter and the snout consequently blunter. Otherwise, especially in their adaptations to an aquatic life, alligators are very similar to crocodiles.

One of the two species is found in North America, the other in China. The Chinese alligator averages a little over 4 ft in length and has no webs between the toes. The American alligator is much larger, with a maximum recorded length of 19 ft 2 in. This length, however, is seldom attained nowadays because the American alligator has been killed off for the sake of its skin; whenever there is intense persecution of an animal the larger ones are quickly

eliminated and the average size of the remainder drops slowly as persecution proceeds.

It is sheer accident that two such similar reptiles as the alligator and the crocodile should so early have been given different common names. The reason is that when the Spanish seamen, who had presumably no knowledge of crocodiles, first saw large reptiles in the Central American rivers, they spoke of them as lizards—el largato *in Spanish. The English sailors who followed later adopted the Spanish name but ran the two into one to make 'allagarter'—which was later further corrupted to 'alligator'.*

Long lazy life
Alligators are more sluggish than crocodiles and this possibly affects their longevity. There are records of alligators having lived for over 50 years. They spend most of their time basking in swamps and on the banks of lakes and rivers.

The American alligator is restricted to the south-eastern United States and does not penetrate further north than latitude 35. The Chinese alligator is found only in the Yangtse River basin.

Meat eaters
Alligators' food changes with age. The young feed on insects and on those crustaceans generally known as freshwater shrimps. As they grow older they eat frogs, snakes and fish; mature adults live mainly on fish but will catch muskrats and small mammals that go down to the water's edge to drink. They also take a certain amount of waterfowl. Very large alligators may

occasionally pull large mammals such as deer or cows down into the water and drown them.

Alligator builds a nest
It seems that the female alligator plays the more active role in courtship and territorial defence. The males apparently spend much of the breeding season quarrelling among themselves, roaring and fighting and injuring each other. The roaring attracts the females to the males, as does a musky secretion from glands in the male's throat and cloaca. Courtship takes place usually at night, the pair swimming round faster and faster and finally mating in the water with jaws interlocked and the male's body arched over the female's.

A large nest-mound is made for the reception of the eggs. The female scoops up mud in her jaws and mixes it with decaying vegetation; the mixture is then deposited on the nest site until a mound 3 ft high is made. The eggs are hard-shelled and number 15–80; they are laid in a depression in the top of the mound and covered with more vegetation. The female remains by the eggs until they hatch 2–3 months later, incubated by the heat of the nest's rotting vegetation.

The hatchling alligators peep loudly and the female removes the layer of vegetation over the nest to help them escape. Baby alligators are 8 in. long when first hatched and grow 1 ft a year, reaching maturity at 6 years.

The biter bitten
Young alligators fall an easy prey to carnivorous fish, birds and mammals, and at all stages of growth they are attacked and eaten

△ *A female alligator builds a nest of rotting vegetation for her clutch of 15—80 eggs. She stays for 2—3 months by the nest until they hatch.*

▽ *Alligators spend much of their time basking in the sun. Here, by their thrashing about, they have made a lagoon by a river.*

by larger alligators. This natural predation was, in the past, just sufficient to keep the numbers of alligator populations steady. Then came the fashion for making women's shoes, handbags and other ornamental goods of alligator skin. So long as these articles remain in fashion and command a high price, men will be prepared to risk both the imprisonment consequent on the laws passed to protect alligators and the attacks of the alligators themselves.

There was also another commercial interest, detrimental both to the alligator and to the fashion industry. For, while the fashion for skins from larger individuals was at its height, a fashion for alligator pets set in. Baby alligators were netted in large numbers for the pet shops, but—as so commonly happens with pets taken from the wild—not all those caught are eventually sold. When a consignment of a large number of hatchlings eventually reaches its destination, many of them are in poor condition and some may be dead and putrefying.

In addition to persecution, land drainage has seriously affected the numbers of the American alligator. The Chinese alligator is an even worse case. Its flesh is eaten and the various parts of its body are used as charms, aphrodisiacs and for their supposed medicinal properties. Although they are kept in zoos, they have not bred as has the American alligator.

Pets down the drain

The fashion for alligator pets had its disadvantages for owners as well as the alligator populations. Even setting aside the maximum recorded lengths for the American species, of 19 ft upwards, it still achieves too large a size to be convenient in the modern flat, and people who invested in an alligator often found it necessary to dispose of it. Zoos proved unable to deal with the quantity offered them—Brookfield Zoo near Chicago built up an enormous herd from unwanted pets. It is often said that unfortunate alligators are disposed of in such a way that they end up in the sewers. Headlines have appeared in the press to the effect that the sewers of New York are teeming with alligators that prey on the rats and terrorize sewermen. However, such reports are greatly exaggerated; cold winters would soon kill them off.

class	**Reptilia**
order	**Crocodilia**
family	**Alligatoridae**
genus & species	***Alligator mississippiensis*** *American alligator*
	A. sinensis *Chinese alligator*

America

America, or the New World, is composed of two land masses, triangular in form, lying north to south, and connected by an isthmus. However, these two land masses were not always connected. Indeed for many millions of years—from the Palaeocene to the middle Pliocene—they were separate. As a result, South America remained entirely isolated; while North America was still able to communicate with Eurasia.

In the Pliocene, the Bering and Panama isthmuses were re-established, allowing exchanges of fauna to take place. Up to this time the mammals of South America had lived in an entirely closed-off area. But by the end of the Pliocene, they were confronted by mammals from North America—and as a result of that confrontation a number of South American species disappeared.

The Americas stretch across the globe from the northern to the southern hemisphere. In other words, they cover all latitudes. Depending on the altitudes at which they lie, these latitudes can be formed into zones, which contain every possible climate and all the great known biomes. A major characteristic of these two linked land masses is a range of mountains that drives southwards from Alaska, all the way to Tierra del Fuego. But there is no such great natural barrier to check migrations from north to south—an important point, and one we will come back to.

Placental mammals developed during the Eocene. It was a warm epoch and all the mammalian orders known today date more or less from this time. Henceforward, the passage of fauna from one land mass to the other would become of prime importance in relation to the intense fluctuations of climate that would follow. These important movements of fauna, after the emergence of the Panama Isthmus, took place in the Pleistocene. For at this time the level of the oceans dropped, due to water being taken up by glaciers which were widely extended throughout the world.

From now on the two Americas need to be regarded as zoogeographically independent. North America is looked upon as the Nearctic region and South America as the Neotropical region, although the latter region extends all the way from central America and the Antilles to Patagonia. At the same time it is worth remembering that the Nearctic region and the Palaearctic region (Europe, temperate Asia and North Africa) are often grouped together as one region—the Holarctic region. In general, the division of the northern hemisphere into two regions is useful, but the number of comparable or closely related species make the Holarctic region a justifiable unity.

Although the New World can be divided into two major regions, Central America forms a stumbling block to this division. For though it is most frequently included in the Neotropical region, it is in fact an area of inter-penetration of land and sea—with varied landscape and climates. The question arises, therefore, as to whether there are two or, in fact, three Americas—and it is an issue over which geographers are divided.

The well-named backbone of America runs the length of both continents along the Pacific coast. So it prevents us from dissociating them too quickly. As we have said, this immense mountain barrier did not prove any impediment to north-south communication—but it has done so between east and west. We will return to this when we deal with climate. It is worth remembering, though, that Africa and South America were once large adjoining blocks of land in the super-continent of Gondwanaland. In the Tertiary they became separated, forming two immense islands that were increasingly pushed apart by movement of oceanic plates.

Configuration and climate

In a sense, the geographical configuration of America is simple. It follows a similar pattern on both continental land masses as a powerful, geologically crumpled, mountain range with high peaks and a scattering of volcanoes, dominates the entire Pacific side. These mountains frame high plateaus, which are wide in North America, between the Rockies and the Sierra Nevada, and more compact in South America along the Cordilleras of the Andes.

After the break up of the supercontinent Pangaea, North America and Eurasia formed the continent of Laurasia until the early Cenozoic era. This accounts for the many faunal characteristics that these two modern land masses have in common.

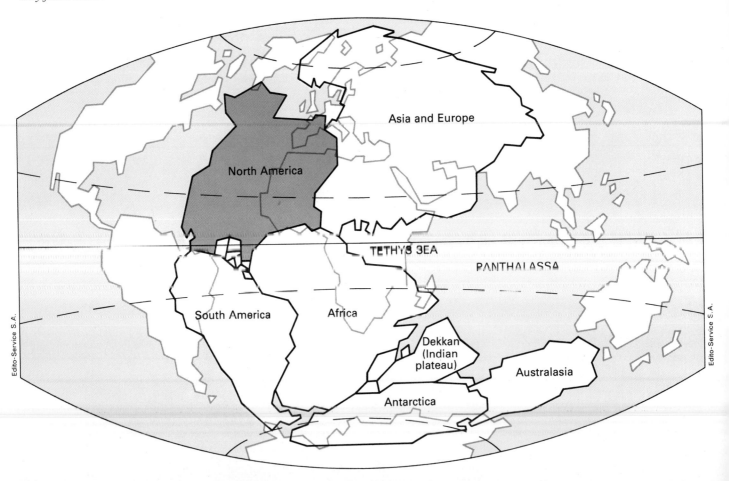

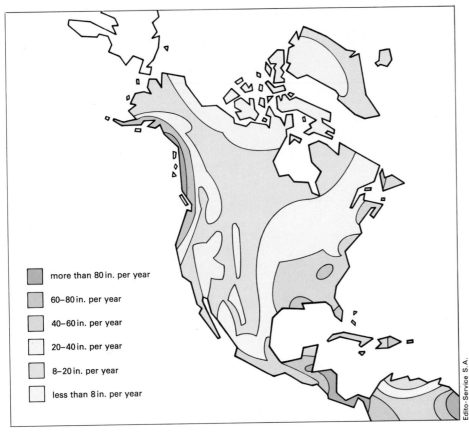

more than 80 in. per year

60–80 in. per year

40–60 in. per year

20–40 in. per year

8–20 in. per year

less than 8 in. per year

The North American climate is decided by the geographical relief of the country. The winds from the Pacific are halted by the Rockies and the country does not have the beneficial influence of an oceanic climate. Large areas are chilled by the cold polar air, or warmed by hot tropical air. The coastal zones are disturbed by marine currents. St. Laurent, at the same latitude as Bordeaux, is blocked by ice from November to May, while Florida suffers a heat equal to that of Senegal.

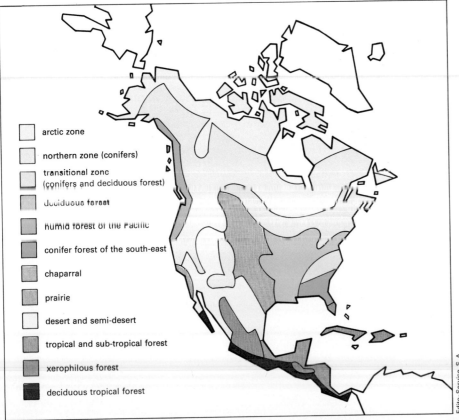

arctic zone

northern zone (conifers)

transitional zone
(conifers and deciduous forest)

deciduous forest

humid forest of the Pacific

conifer forest of the south-east

chaparral

prairie

desert and semi-desert

tropical and sub-tropical forest

xerophilous forest

deciduous tropical forest

The Atlantic side of the continents, planed down by erosion, has what is thought to be the oldest land in the world–the high plateaus of the St. Lawrence and the Appalachians in the north and those of Guyana and Brazil in the south.

On both continents, between their east and west configurations, there are enormous plains–prairies and savannas in the north; llanos, pampas and chaco in the south. This may appear simplistically diagrammatic, but on a large scale that is exactly how the geographical configuration of the two continents lies.

It is always interesting to see how continental and maritime influences affect particular regions. A large part of the thermal energy accumulated by the oceans is recycled into the atmosphere and contributes to the appearance of meteorological disturbances. A barrier of high mountains can stop clouds, and regions located at the same latitudes in different parts of the world are generally incomparable in terms of climate. New York, at the same latitude as Naples, has a January mean temperature 10°C/18°F below that of the Italian city. As great a difference exists between equatorial America and Africa in July.

Atmospheric circulation

Between the eastern and western high lands of the two continents run what can be seen as vast corridors. These favour the penetration of cold winds from the north. Given different names in each region they cross, these winds blow as far south as Argentina–where they are known as 'pamperos'.

On other continents there is generally free atmospheric circulation from west to east. But the barrier of the two Cordilleras prevents this in South America. As a result, the influence of the Pacific Ocean–which might otherwise regulate or soften the climate into a more temperate one–cannot come fully into play.

The mass of its geographical configurations, and the way in which they are arranged, determines a continent's general atmospheric conditions. Local topography also has an important influence on temperature. But all sorts of specific regions can be influenced by different factors. The north of Chile, for instance, has desert which results more from the cold Humboldt current than any general dynamics. In Venezuela, land is cultivated up to altitudes of 11 000 ft. The independent action of other geographical and climatic factors will always be superimposed on any latitudinal picture.

Trade winds, monsoons and currents

America lies under the influence of two great planetary systems of atmospheric circulation: monsoons and trade winds. Central America, which is so relatively narrow, provides a good example of the effect of these trades. On the Caribbean coast, they bring rain. On the Pacific coast, though, the climate, in contrast, has less winter rainfall–and, most importantly, no tropical cyclones.

The factors that combine to form any given territory are complex and considerable–and we will deal with them in specific instances when they relate to some unusual aspect of a region. As well as their influence on the Americas today, the trade winds have

Edito-Service S.A.

Edito-Service S.A.

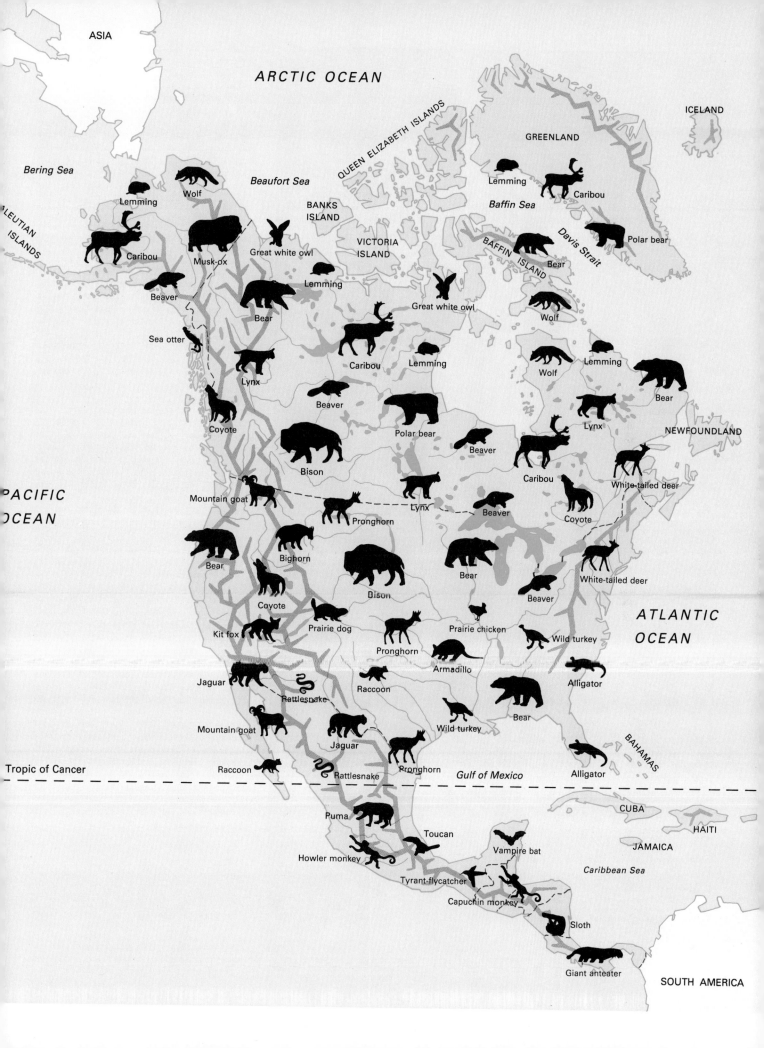

an historical importance. For they made possible the discovery of the New World in the 16th century.

The opposition of America's great continental and oceanic masses produces a form of monsoon, a phenomenon most marked in the region of the Gulf of Mexico. This warm 'interior sea' has an altogether considerable influence on the climate of a large part of the United States.

A number of oceanic currents also contribute to the contradictory nature of the American climate. They act directly on the coasts that receive them—and either warm or cool them as a result.

Animal distribution

We could view the animals of America in terms of its different geographical regions; try to list all the species that are found in each; cover every animal of the tundra and all the creatures that live in the desert. But this would take up too much space, so the major vegetation zones will be covered, and only those animals of major importance will be dealt with.

Tundra

America can be seen as having two regions of tundra. One in the north, the other at the far south of South America, where it might be considered as entering the Antarctic circle. Tundra can be defined as barren, almost perpetually frozen, land. As such, it is found in Alaska, Canada and those parts of Greenland not covered by ice. It supports a few species, but those that do exist are represented by a large number of individuals—as its huge swarms of mosquitoes in summer exemplify.

Some tundra animals

North American tundra is the home of the caribou *Rangifer tarandus* (p. 512), which is now protected, and the musk-ox *Ovibus moschatus* (p. 1687), which was once common, but is now confined to certain parts of Canada and Greenland. Rodents of this tundra include lemmings (p. 1431), such as Greenland's collared lemming *Dicrostonyx groenlandicus*, Barrow ground Squirrel *Citellus parryi* (p. 1108), the shrew-mouse *Sorex cinerus*, as well as the stoat or ermine *Mustella erminea* (p. 2400) and the American mink *Mustela vison* (p. 1617). In Alaska, more particularly, one finds two voles, *Clethrionomys retilus* and *Microtus oeconomus*. The polar or Arctic hare *Lepus arcticus*, the grey marmot *Marmota caligata* and the Arctic fox *Alopex lagopus* (p. 174) are also creatures that manage to survive and reproduce in this inhospitable region.

The American marmot. Its area of distribution extends from Labrador to Novia Scotia, towards the south to Virginia and Alabama, towards the west to Kansas, crossing Minnesota and central Canada to the Rocky Mountains.

The red, or pine, squirrel Tamiasciurus douglasii, *of North America; one of two species called chickarees because of their call when disturbed.*

The tundra has a considerable number and variety of birds. Among them are the great northern diver *Gavia immer* (p. 774), the Canada goose *Branta canadensis* (p. 490), the great snow goose *Anser caerulescens*, the emperor goose *A. canagicus*, the king eider *Somateria spectabilis* (p. 833) and the rock ptarmigan *Lagopus mutus* (p. 1995). The Arctic tern *Sterna paradisea* (p. 2503) is found here as well, and so are the long-tailed skua *Stercorarius longicaudus* (p. 2275), the white-winged gull *Larus glaucoides*, some types of sandpiper, the red phalarope *Phalaropus fulicarius* (p. 1881), the grey plover *Pluvialis squatarola* (p. 1933), the great snowy owl *Nyctea scandiaca* (p. 2312), and the snow bunting *Plectrophenax nivalis* (p. 447). The American golden plover *Plurialis dominica* (p.

1933) nests in the north of Canada (also in Alaska and Siberia). But in the autumn it flies–non-stop–all the way to Hawaii, and then farther south still. The Alaskan or bristle-thighed curlew *Numenius arquata* (p. 728) has a similar pattern of behaviour, flying far across the Pacific to winter in Polynesia.

Fauna of the taiga
Conifers grow from the south of Alaska and Canada right down to the north-western seaboard of the United States. This immense region of forest (which, though not as hostile as the tundra, still has a very harsh climate) is known as taiga. In Canada alone it occupies an area estimated at 1 000 000 000 acres.

Following on progressively from the tundra, the taiga eventually gives way to deciduous forest in the south. Throughout its considerable extent (with very slight local variations) it is strikingly uniform–and never uninhabited, even in winter. A number of birds can be found here and the mammals of the taiga (unlike tundra mammals, such as reindeer, which can abandon their normal habitat to shelter in the taiga forest) never leave it.

Rodents found here include the chipmunks (p. 566), which are rather like small ground squirrels with large cheek pockets; two different kinds of red squirrel; ground (or rock) squirrels, which crop up again in Asia–and three species of native squirrel. Of these, the chickaree *Tamiasciurus hudsonicus*

Musk-oxen Ovibus moschatus *are very big, standing 5 ft at the shoulder and weighing up to 700 lbs.*

(p. 553) is worth special mention as it winters in the north of its area of distribution. A large marten called the fisher (p. 1568) and Gapper's vole also live in the taiga—as do hare (p. 1153), American mink (p. 1617), weasel (p. 2689), American marten (p. 1568), red fox (p. 2063), lynx (p. 1488), wolverine (p. 2735) and brown bear (p. 426).

Bears

Bears are widely distributed throughout the northern hemisphere—and not found at all in the southern. Except, that is, for the spectacled bear *Tremarctos ornatus* (p. 2340), which is a uniquely South American species.

Far to the north, the Kodiak bear *Ursus arctos middendorff* is found specifically on Kodiak Island off Alaska. This race of brown bear is a giant. Up to 9 ft tall it is a vegetarian for most of the year, living off plants and roots—but in the spring catches salmon on their migration runs to spawn in river tributaries.

The grizzly bear has the reputation of being the most ferocious of all bears. It may well be. But, in the animal world, such things can vary considerably according to the individual and the region. The grizzly *U. a. horribilis* is another sub-species of brown bear. The American black bear *U. americanus* (p. 361) is also an inhabitant of the taiga. It has a number of sub-species, which can be found from Canada to Mexico.

Lynx and mustelids

The Canada lynx *Lynx canadensis* (p. 1488) is a true creature of the far north, and with its large and calloused paws is perfectly adapted to the territories in which it lives.

Mustelids are widely distributed in North America. The American mink can be found throughout northern regions and so can the pygmy weasel *Mustela nivalis rixosa*. The American marten *Martes americana* lives in wooded parts of Canada, Newfoundland and Alaska. The fisher, a large marten species, has similar, though apparently less northern, distribution, while the Canadian otter *Lutra canadensis* (p. 1784) ranges, in fact, through the entire American north, and can be seen as far south as the southern United States.

Canada

Canada is one of the largest countries in the world. It takes up half of the North American land mass and encompasses three major climatic zones: polar, sub-polar and mid-latitude. The sub-polar region, however, represents two-thirds of the country's total surface, and its summers are brief.

Mountain puma (p. 2009) and wapiti (p. 2659), Canada's deer, were once abundant in the forests of its Pacific coast. These forests still preserve their decidedly northern character. The entire country is marked by an ice age that only ended 12 000 years ago—

The northern lynx Lynx lynx *hunts at night using its particularly keen sight and may follow scent trails for miles.*

which is very recently on the geological time scale. Canada has a disorganized system of rivers and lakes as a result. Tangled watercourses thread their way with difficulty through terrain that still bears the imprint of glaciation–jumbles of moraine and ice-smoothed, ice-borne and abandoned rock.

Canada's alpine regions with their neighbouring glaciers resemble Arctic tundra. But their deeper soil and more variable temperatures give rise, even here, to areas of grass capable of supporting wild sheep (p 336), mountain goats (p. 2018) and the mountain beaver *Aplodontia rufa* (p. 2220).

Very broadly speaking, Canada can be summed up as a country of forests, prairies, and vast Alpine zones. Its prairies are not yet the great grassy plains of the United States. However corn is grown in the South of Manitoba. While in the east, Canada's northern coniferous forest gives way to deciduous forest–with the maples of Ontario and the St Lawrence, and the elm and ash that border the watercourses of its plains.

Canadian fauna

The wolverine *Gulo gulo* (p. 2735) inhabits the 138 square miles of Canada's British Columbia. In winter it preys on elk and reindeer; but it does not really merit its alternative name of glutton–as its stomach is only capable of containing 4 lb of food.

Lemmings (p. 1431) are northern animals and, not counting the Hudson collared lemming *Dicrostonyx hudsonius*, there are four species in North America: *Synaptomys cooperi*, *S. borealis*, *Lemmus trimucronatus* and *L. nigreps*.

The muskrat *Ondatra zibethica* (p. 1690) grows to the size of a rabbit. It originated in the New World–from which it has colonized the Old–and is very widely distributed throughout North America. The American jumping mice of northern Canada are worth pointing out. Two species, *Zapus hudsonius* and *Z. trinotatus*, live in Canada's Pacific regions, while two other species live farther south.

The only North American porcupine, *Erethizon dorsatum*, would be an easy creature to overlook, for it has solitary ways. Although found in other areas, its distribution is sufficiently northern for it to be mentioned here.

Surprisingly, the north has its bats as well. The northern bat *Lasiurus borealis* and the ashy bat *L. cinerus* (see p. 2633) are relatively recent arrivals and almost certainly not as accustomed to cold as the two-toned serotine (which even lives in Arctic zones). All the same, they are found high in the region of the Hudson Bay–though they leave to spend the winter in the south of the United States.

Forests

Northern forests are often loosely grouped under the single word taiga. Though, strictly speaking, the term only refers to one of their

The wolverine Gulo gulo, *the largest member of the weasel family, depends for its survival on driving other predators away from their food.*

J.-P. Varin – Jacana

Coniferous forests cover large areas of Canada and the Rocky Mountains.

northerly aspects and as they go south they change. This northern forest is immense—the largest continuous forest in the world, in fact. (In contrast taiga proper should be considered as essentially of the very far north—with relatively wide-spaced trees and soil covered with moss and lichen below them.)

The great northern forests of the Rockies should be distinguished from the Hudson forest; their extraordinary extent of conifers starts on the West coast in Alaska and the Yukon—almost as far north as the sixty-fifth parallel—only reaches its peak in British Columbia, and extends down into California, where it finally ends. This is the Pacific conifer forest.

The Hudson forest on the other hand, is essentially North Canadian. It encompasses the most rugged and beautiful landscapes, where lakes and pools (formed by prehistoric periods of glaciation) mirror virgin nature. Including the Canadian 'musteg' with its vast stretches of peat, the Hudson forest consists of several varieties of tree which result from differences in soil and rainfall. But it is quite usual, in some places, to find only a single kind of tree—and entire regions of forest can be found of balsam fir (*Abies balsamea*) alone. (The buds of this fir go to make Canadian balsam—and the caterpillar

of *Choristoneura fumiferana* is extremely fond of them.) Overall, spruce dominates in the Hudson forest which covers a wide band of territories stretching east; while on the inland side of the Rocky Mountains, at the foot of cliffs which date from the Pre-Cambrian era, one finds thick conifer forests—widely interspersed with lovely mountain grasslands.

The forests of the Appalachians and St Lawrence

The vast forest of the St Lawrence region to the south of the great Canadian plains, consists mainly of conifer. But farther south, maple, oak and hornbeam predominate with birch on poor soil—and one comes to the forests of the Appalachians, a luxuriant woodland of deciduous trees, like oak, chestnut, maple and beech.

These forests bring us to a description of the vegetation of the Atlantic coast that will apply as far south as Florida. In the extreme north the east coast consists of a region of sub-Arctic tundra. A transitional zone follows. Then, in succession, come the forests of the Hudson, the St Lawrence and the Appalachians. These are then followed by a type of forest known as 'Chinese'.

Ecologically speaking, these forests are all

extremely important. They provide a habitat for a great variety of animals—and the American moose, lynx, black bear, beaver, red squirrel and marmot are all typical of northern forests. Just as the wolf, caribou, wolverine and varying hare are typical of the sub-Arctic zone.

'Chinese' forest is found in territories that extend from the lower Mississippi to South Carolina, and include Florida. It is called 'Chinese' because of its different varieties, which compare with southern China. In essence these are forests of large-leaved evergreens or laurel woods, which continue into deciduous temperate forests (found in regions of the United States with mild winters of not less than 8°C/46°F).

The Appalachian forests begin at a latitude of 45°, where the climate is quite cold and rainy. The St Lawrence forests start further north and extend above the Great Lakes up to Gaspésie National Park where they begin to mingle with great conifers. The annual mean temperature of this region is a low one, though its summers can still be a comfortable 20°C/68°F. The Hudson forest, in turn, extends from Labrador to James Bay and beyond.

Without going into more detail, these are the principal types of northern American

The Virginia deer is found in both North and South America. It generally lives alone or in small groups.

forest. Their description was important, not only because it gives some idea of the continent's landscape, but also because it helps to define the distribution of much of its fauna–and fix animals in their appropriate habitats.

The temperate north

In terms of climate, North America can be broadly divided in two: Canada to the north; the United States and Mexico to the south. The continent's temperate regions are considered to correspond to the area occupied by the United States. As on other continents, fauna becomes more rich and varied the more one goes south. In Alaska, for instance, there are at most 30 species of mammals. But by the time one reaches Arizona, that figure has risen to 140.

There are very few true temperate climates in the world, however. (To be temperate a climate must have marked differences between seasons and variable weather within those seasons themselves). Except in narrow coastal areas, few continents have regions of any size that correspond to this climate as exemplified in Western Europe. So, although the United States is considered to occupy North America's temperate region, this distinction is quite arbitrary. So-called temper-

ate forests can begin too high in Canada, for instance, and climatically comparable bands even occur in the southern hemisphere.

Large mammals

Vast herds of American bison *Bison bison* (p. 353) once roamed the Canadian prairies. But today these flat central regions between the forests and mountains of the east and west are largely cultivated, their watercourses bordered with poplar and willow. Yet they still provide a home for many birds that live there permanently, as well as a vital migratory zone for all sorts of species of geese, grebe and duck.

Like bison, wapiti (p. 2659) once lived on the plains. They no longer do so, but still number 6 sub-species (which are poorly defined and contested by zoologists), among them a pygmy breed that lives in California. Along with the bison, brown bear, wolf and beaver, wapiti originally came to North America from Asia via land links that existed in prehistoric times. They were named wapiti by the Red Indians in the days when they inhabited the plains; and now live in open forest, from which they go up into the mountains in summer–to return again, come winter, to low-lying regions. The species with the largest numbers is the Rocky Moun-

tain wapiti *Cervus elephas nelsoni*.

The Virginia deer *Odocoileus virginianus* (p. 1671) also known as the white-tailed deer, has a large number of sub-species. The heavier breeds live in the north, and further south they tend to diminish in size. The mule deer *O. hemionus* is only found in North American mountains and has a sub-species that is peculiar to the Rockies. The black-tailed deer lives in clearings and under-growth. Of all these, only the Virginian deer can adapt to modifications in environments as the result of cultivation.

Like the almost annihilated bison, the pronghorn *Antilocapra americana* (p. 1993), which looks like an antelope but is given its own family due to certain physical features, was once numbered in millions. Almost entirely wiped out, the few thousand remaining were protected just in time–and it has returned, between the Missouri and the Rocky Mountains, in some hundreds of thousands.

Some zoologists consider that all bison have a common origin (*Bison sivalensis*) and that European and American bison are sub-species of the same animal; others think they are morphologically and anatomically differentiated species. Whatever may be the case, it is worth pointing out that the differ-

The Rocky Mountain goat Oreamnos americanus *is related to the European and Asian chamois. It lives in the high mountains of the north.*

Kojo Tanaka

ence between prairie and forest bison is that the latter are the larger of the two.

The Rocky Mountain goat *Oreamnos americanus* (p. 2108) is related to the chamois of Europe and Asia, and today lives in US national parks. Its true homeland, however, is in the Canadian Rockies, and several thousand still live there. Excellent climbers, these goats in general prefer to remain in the higher regions of their mountains above the tree-line. Bighorns *Ovis canadensis* (p 336), which are a breed of tough mountain sheep with magnificent curled horns, can be found in similar regions.

Mustelidae

The American badger *Taxidea taxus* (p. 274) can be found from Canada all the way to Mexico—even on dry plains. It has a flat-shaped body and long fur; and in its most northern habitats will hibernate during the winter.

The American continent has a variety of skunks (p. 2278): the striped skunk, *Mephitis mephitis*, is found as far north as southern Canada; the spotted skunk, *Spilogale putorius*, is in general more southerly, though both are found in the United States and Mexico. The hooded skunk, *M. macroura*, lives in North and Central America, and skunks can be found as far south as the Magellan Straits. In general, spotted skunks inhabit rocky regions, while the others favour forest or prairies. The skunk is a small flesh-eating animal with a silky coat, and is renowned for the vile odour it can eject from its anal scent glands—as a most effective means of defence.

America has three species of otter (p. 1784) that correspond to its major geographical divisions: the Canadian or North American otter, *Lutra canadensis*, the Central American otter, *L. annecteus*, and the South American otter, *L. paltensis*. South America has at least four other species as well, and the otter sub-family, the Lutrinae, includes about 18 species that are found throughout the globe. Otters are aquatic, but their diet is not confined to fish and they will eat vole and muskrat as well. The marine otter, *Enhydra lutris* which lives off the North Pacific coasts, is famous for being a tool user. It lies on the ocean surface and uses a rock to smash open the sea urchins and clams on which it feeds. Due to public concern and action by conservationists the marine otter has been saved from extinction.

True Americans

Most members of the family Procyonidae belong to the New World alone; and the ring-tailed cat, also known as the North American cacomistle or cunning cat-squirrel, *Bassariscus astutus* (p. 479), is typical of them. Other members of the family, often referred to as the 'little bear' family, include the raccoons (p. 2032), coatis (p. 592), kinkajous (p. 1369) and pandas (p. 1824). Only the pandas are not American. All are omnivorous plantigrades, however, and all, with one exception (the giant panda), have long tails.

The ring-tailed cat can be confused with the raccoon; but it is sleeker and its black-ringed tail is longer than its body. Living in the west of the United States and Central America, it is the most primitive representative of its family (which, for reasons of appearance, is positioned between the Mustelidae and Ursidae). It is a cunning animal, as its Latin name of *Bassaricus astutus* suggests.

There are various sub-species of ring-tailed cat which all have slightly different habitats; though their main one (for the northern breed) consists of any dry and rocky region in which they can be found from California to Mexico. (In direct contrast, the sub-species *B. a. sumichrasti*, lives in the humid forests of Central America.)

Raccoons have a reputation for invariably immersing their food in water before they eat it, as has been observed in captive raccoons. But in their natural state they do not always do this—as, for a start, they often catch aquatic prey. An interesting example, this, of how an animal's behaviour in captivity can mislead one as to how it lives in the wild.

There are a number of sub-species of North American raccoon *Procyon lotor*, some of them quite small. Their ancestral line is represented by one with thick grey-brown fur, which makes its body look larger than it

80

The bighorn Ovis canadensis *of western North America. Their coats are of coarse hair and not woolly like their descendant, the domestic sheep.*

actually is. Ranging from 20 in. to 40 in. in size, they are nocturnal and good swimmers. They are sometimes found quite far north, where they hibernate in winter. In the south the crab-eating raccoon *Procyon cancrivorus* turns up even in mangrove swamps. The island raccoons that live in the islands off Florida are also worth pointing out, and a pygmy breed is found in Central America.

The brown coati *Nasua narica* appears from the western United States on, but is mainly found in Central America—and we will discuss coatis when we consider that region.

The origin of the dog
The family Canidae contains those fissiped (separate toed) carnivores which have *Canis*, the dog, as their archetype. They may well have a North American origin dating from the beginning of the Tertiary period, and fossils have been found of a comparable creature with a poorly developed brain—but possessing the distinguishing five-toed hind feet. This first ancestor may well have given rise to a flourishing family (the Borophagidae) in what is today the United States, and although these creatures are now extinct, they call to mind some contemporary breeds of dog.

Some experts, however, dispute this. For them the domestic dog remains a zoological enigma, the wild species from which it issued being unknown. The general picture is not simplified either by the fact that, while some

maintain that wolves and jackals can cross with dogs and produce fertile offspring, others absolutely deny this.

The origin of the dog, in short, is controversial. Archaeologists claim that there were domestic dogs some 10 000 years ago in Asia, Egypt, Europe and North America, and that, in each one of these regions, there was more than one breed. Some experts designate the ancestor of all these already-domesticated dogs as *Tomarctus*, which was a short-legged predator. But the question which remains to be resolved is whether all the domestications of this animal occurred at one time, or quite independently in several places. Again, other experts believe the domestic dog had *three* probable ancestors—and that it came about through a series of crosses. Others think, quite simply, that the domestic dog is descended from the wolf.

Somewhere or other, there must have been an initial ancestral line, which then divided into other lines, three of which have survived up to now: sub-families Caninae (dogs, foxes, wolves, jackals), Cyoninae (bush dog, hunting dog) and Otocyoninae (bat-eared fox)—a diversity of species that can be attributed to a great range of hereditary factors. At any rate, if these canids did first appear in North America, they were certainly ideally placed to colonize the Old World via the Bering Isthmus, South America via Panama—and this colonization most probably took place in successive waves.

The Canidae
The family Canidae today encompasses many genera—*Canis, Alopex, Vulpes, Fennecus* and a large number of species.

The wolf is found in Europe, Asia and North America. The dingo was introduced into Australia as a domestic animal by man and then went wild. While, in America, coyotes perform the ecological function of jackals on other continents. (From the Mesolithic on, the domestic dog became so diversified it requires a separate study: see p. 780.)

The common wolf (p. 2729) still lives in considerable numbers in Canada and Alaska, and there are a few in the United States. North American wolves fall into three general categories: forest wolves, which are black; the great north wolf, which is grey-white; and the brown wolf *Canis lupus niger* which is the very image of the species and originates in the southern United States. All wolves are natural enemies of the coyote.

Coyotes *C. latrans* (p. 682) can be met virtually everywhere in the North American countryside. They adapt easily, and forced out of one region by man's efforts to exterminate them, will move into another.

The European red fox *Vulpes vulpes* (p. 2063) is found throughout the northern hemisphere; but the sub-species *V. v. fulva*, or tawny fox, is exclusively North American. It is related to the big-eared fox *V. macrotis* and the kit fox *V. velox*. Two species of the great

△ *The kit fox can move very rapidly when attacking, but flees by making unexpected zig-zags.*

▽ *The coyote used to live in western America but now they are found from Alaska to North America.*

Albert Visage – Jacana

Ph. Mallet – Jacana

American West, their distribution begins in south-west Canada and extends right down past Texas and New Mexico. The big-eared fox weighs no more than 6½ lb and happily hunts at night. The kit fox is adapted for desert and sub-desert life, being extremely quick over short distances.

The silver fox is a hybrid form of tawny fox, bred by man for its beautiful fur. It should not be confused with the grey fox of the genus *Urocyon* (p. 1099) which lives in central and northern South America.

The plains of the United States

Many of the animals we have so far mentioned live, or once lived, on American plains and it is worth considering just what these animals are.

As we have seen, the major geographical configurations of the American continent are orientated north-to-south. And between the Appalachians to the east and the Rockies to the west, is a great central, low-lying region of plains that extend for hundreds of miles. But there are also plains in the Great Lakes region; in Mississippi and Missouri; at the foot of the Rocky Mountains; and bordering the Gulf of Mexico—not to mention those of the Atlantic seaboard.

In general, all these plains are cultivated. They are therefore an environment created and ordered by man. As a result, few mammals are able to live there on a permanent basis: they merely come to these regions from neighbouring habitats to find their food. Small rodents have a better chance than most of establishing themselves, but their success largely depends on an area's particular type of cultivation. Small animals that do not live in the ground can be effectively fettered by sudden variations in crops. As a general rule, then, the species that live in widely cultivated zones are rare.

The family of ground squirrels (p. 1108) is among this small number. Related to tree squirrels, they are earth-living rodents and include the Columbian ground squirrel *Citellus columbianus*, which attacks cereals, and Richardson's ground squirrel *C. richardsoni* which feeds on grass crops. Rabbits of course can survive here too and cottontails (p. 671) do considerable damage in winter.

North American rodents and their habitats

North American lagomorphs live in a wide variety of environments. The northern hare inhabits both evergreen forests and marshy regions with trees. The white-tailed jack rabbit *Lepus townsendii* (p. 1314), despite its name, is a hare and lives not only on the great prairies, but also in mountains up to heights of more than 13 000 ft. Some long-haired species live just as well in the western and Mexican deserts as on the plains. The black tailed jack rabbit *L. californicus* is widespread throughout the western United States. The antelope jack rabbit *L. alleni* is well adapted to deserts, and the white-sided jack rabbit *L. mexicanus* inhabits the high plateaus of its country.

The pygmy rabbit *Brachylagus idahoensis* lives in the Sierra Nevada. The eastern cottontail *Sylvilagus floridanus* (p. 671) adjusts well to civilization—perhaps too well. The brush rabbit *S. bachmani* is Californian. Others inhabit marshy zones. On the Gulf of

Mexico seaboard, there is the marsh or swamp rabbit *S. aquaticus*, which frequents swampy areas and enters water readily and swims well. The eastern cottontail lives on the Atlantic coast of Mexico, and though both the eastern cottontail and the brush rabbit are found in the same range, the first lives in low regions, the second in more elevated and marshy ones, and so they do not cohabit or compete for living space.

Pocket gophers (p. 1941) are a truly North American family of rodents. There are 30 species and they spend the greater part of their life underground. Their principal genera include *Geomys, Thomomys, Cratogeomys, Zygogeomys* and *Macrogeomys*.

Pumas

The puma *Puma concolor* (p. 2009) once inhabited all America from north to south, but today has been driven back into the west. It is said to like rocky, well-forested regions, but perhaps it has been forced to by the ceaseless vendetta ranchers wage against it. The puma's existence is constantly threatened and yet it has an extraordinary faculty for adaptation. It can live in northern forest, mountains, plains, and is even found in the tropical forest of Brazil. Hunted it may be, but it is surviving—and in a number of places there is a growing appreciation of its contribution to the balance of nature.

The horse

It would be a gross omission to speak of America without mentioning horses. For the horse still makes an important contribution to the life of many American states today. Historically speaking, this has a certain justice to it, for it was the Europeans who reintroduced the horse to North America, where it had disappeared—as it had from South America as a result of the last ice age.

The horse is an ungulate: ungulates being a heterogenous group of animals. The evolution of the horse took place over a period of some 60 000 000 years—mainly in North America. This evolution can be followed quite precisely from the beginning of the Tertiary period and occurred in three distinct directions, which affected size, teeth and limbs. In the Oligocene epoch, the *Anchitherium* (a type of forest reindeer) spread throughout Asia and Europe. Some of its Miocene descendents adapted to life on the steppes and produced the genus *Merychippus*. At the end of the Miocene, this branch in turn evolved the genus *Hipparion*. Later, in the Pleistocene, came the genus *Equus*—from which all present-day species have sprung (see p. 1243).

Peccary

Wild pigs never colonized the New World. But peccaries (p. 1859), which are not closely related to them, can be found in America from the south of the United States to the Argentine. Some pig species have been introduced too. The collared peccary, *Tayassu tajacu*, lives in mountainous canyons and scrub and is a vegetarian.

Temperate region birds

The temperate regions of the North American land mass offer a variety of both local, and more cosmopolitan, species of birds. Tits (p. 2535), in particular, are well represented

Brosselin – Jacana

△ *The jack rabbit's unusually large ears give it extremely acute hearing.*

▽ *The overwhelming curiosity of a puma often compels it to stalk people, but it rarely attacks.*

Juan Saloro – Jacana

through the sub-family of Parinae, but are called chickadees in North America. North America has only one member of the Remizidae family, which is the golden tit *Auriparus flaviceps*.

Nuthatches (p. 1734), such as the Canadian nuthatch *Sitta canadensis* and the Carolina nuthatch, are well distributed and in places even meet up, although the Carolina nuthatch lives chiefly in leafy forests, while the Canadian favours conifers. Two smaller species are the pygmy nuthatch *S. pygmaea*, which lives in the west, and the brown-headed nuthatch *S. pusilla* of south-eastern pine forests. The common tree creeper *Certhia familiaris* is the only North American treecreeper.

There are ten species of North American small woodpecker called flickers (p. 933), most being brownish or golden-yellow birds with black markings and some red spots. The yellow-shafted flicker *Colaptes auratus*, a northern bird, has several sub-species which between them cover North America—apart from the far north. Other flickers are found in South America. Of the larger woodpeckers (p. 2755), those best established include the pileated woodpecker *Dryocopus pileatus*, which lives in forests, and acorn woodpeckers of the genus *Melanerps*, of which there are 20 American species. The red-headed woodpecker *Melanerps erythrocephalus* is the most northerly. In contrast, the acorn woodpecker *M. formicivorus* lives in California. It supplements insect food with nuts, drilling acorn-sized holes in tree trunks and storing an acorn or nut in each, to eat when insects are scarce. Sapsucker woodpeckers are mainly represented in North America by the spotted woodpecker *Sphyrapicus varius*. But there are a large number of sub-species: all have tiny hairs at the end of their tongues which help them suck out sap from trees.

North American forest thrushes belong to the genus *Hylocichla*. The forest thrushes occupy a good part of the United States. The hermit thrush *H. guttata* is found from Alaska to Virginia; and its relation, the tawny thrush *H. fuscescens* from Canada to the centre of the United States.

Cardinals, tanagers and warblers

Cardinals (p. 508), so called on account of their red plumage, are found throughout the whole continent. The cardinal or red bird *Cardinalis cardinalis* lives in the Mississippi valley; the grey-faced cardinal or pyrrhuloxia *Pyrrhuloxia sinuata* lives in the southern United States and throughout Mexico. The big bodied, red chested thrush tanager *Rhodinocichla rosea* is found in Mexico and Venezuela.

Warblers (p. 2762) are represented in America by two sub-families, which are

△ Dryocopus martins. *Woodpeckers of the genus Dryocopus are found in both North America and Europe.*

◁ *The common treecreeper is found in Britain and in North America where it is known as the browncreeper. It uses grass, moss and leaves to make its nest.*

known as 'sylvettes' and sugar-makers. The northern part also provides a home (far from its nesting region) for the worm-eating blue-winged warbler *Vermivora pinus* and its close relation, the golden-winged warbler *V. chrysoptera*–which are both established south of the Great Lakes and frequently hybridize.

The family Pariludae is generally insectivorous. But one of its warblers, the crowned sylvette *Dendroica coronata* eats bay leaves and the seeds of plants. The protonotary warbler *Protonotaria citrea* lives in marshy forests (in the east); the yellow warbler *D. petechia* in willows and thickets; the ash-headed warbler *D. magnolia* in conifer forests. The crowned warbler, for its part, is a migrator and in winter leaves the Mississippi region for South America.

Vireos (p. 2638) fall into two groups which favour two quite different regions of America. The genus *Vireo* lives in the north, the genus *Hylophilus* in the south. The United States vireos winter in Central America from Mexico onwards, though the red-eyed vireo *V. olivaceus* migrates as far as the Amazon region.

The family Icteridae have a South American ancestry but have also penetrated to North America. The brown-headed cowbird *Molothrus ater* (p. 678) is one of the best adapted, though in winter it will seek a warmer climate, either in the south of Mexico or Florida.

Finches are naturally widespread in North America, and in many places have also been introduced. The common raven *Corvus corax* (p. 2051) was once consistently distributed from Canada right down to the Middle West. Although it still exists in reasonable numbers, its distribution today is quite patchy.

There are two species of wild turkey (p. 2608). The North American common turkey *Meleagris gallopavo* is the ancestor of the domestic turkey and is said to have been brought to Europe by the Conquistadores. The ocellated turkey *Agriocharis ocellata* lives in Guatemala and the lowlands of the Yucatan peninsula.

Vultures

American vultures (see p. 2612) belong to the primitive family of Cathartidae, Eurasian vultures to the family Accipitridae (see p. 2645). The two are entirely separate and only share superficial characteristics and likenesses, brought on by convergent evolution. In fact, anatomical differences between them are quite marked. To mention just one differentiating feature, for instance, vultures of the New World have porous nostrils that communicate with their beaks. All told there are seven species of American vultures–and all are excellent examples of

Dubois – Jacana

Eric Hosking

△ *The raven* Corvus corax *has a wide range in North Amerca and Eurasia. Both parents feed the nestlings for 5–6 weeks.*

▷ *Cardinals are North American birds that formerly lived deep in the forests. However, they have adapted to the presence of man and can now be found in parks and gardens.*

The king vulture Sarcorhamphus papa *lives in the forested areas of Central and South America. It is said to be capable of finding its food by sense of smell, which is rare among birds.*

large birds that are very well adapted to gliding flight. The impressive king vulture is distinguished by its brown and white plumage and still more by its naked head, where orange and red blend with red and mauve. The black vulture *Coragyps atratus* is the smallest North American vulture, and the red-headed turkey vulture *Catharthes aura* is widespread throughout the country.

The condor (p. 644) is one of the largest birds that can fly. In North America there is the California condor *Gymnogyps californianus*; South America has the Andean condor *Vultur gryphus*.

Smaller birds of prey

The smaller American birds of prey are found in a great variety of habitats. The little elf owl *Micrathene whitneyi*, for instance, can be seen in the desert or in forests of pine and oak. In contrast, the caracara falcon *Polyborus cheriway* stays in the direct vicinity of wooded roads and feeds on animals that have been run over by cars.

The great horned owl *Bubo virginianus* is, in general, smaller than the European horned owl and has a number of sub-species of varying size and coloration. It does not usually migrate. (The other members of its genus tend to move south in winter–though not very far.) A nocturnal predator, the great horned owl is widespread throughout the Americas.

The sparrowhawk owl lives in the extreme north of Canada. But it can become erratic and is sometimes found in the far south of Canada as well–which is also the home of the tiny boreal or Tengmalm's owl *Aegolius funereus*. All told, the genus *Aegolius* has four species. The saw-whet owl *A. acadius* lives in the same sort of areas of North America as Tengmalm's owl, though other saw-whet owls are found as far south as Brazil.

Nightjars

Nightjars (p. 1718) can be found throughout the Americas. The main–and most vocal–one is the whip-poor-will *Caprimulgus vociferus* (p. 1963) whose cry defines the limits of its territory; its call is said to sound like its common name. In summer it nests in the western forests of North America; in winter it goes south to Mexico and Central America. The poor-will *Phalaenoptilus nuttalli* lives more to the west, along the Pacific coast. The nighthawk *Chordeiles minor* is comparable to the European nightjar and lives in America at a similar latitude. It may migrate towards the tropics in very cold winters, but exactly where is not known.

The whip-poor-will Caprimulgus vociferus *is named after its call, and appears to hold the record for continuity (1088 calls in succession).*

The white-necked nighthawk *Nyctidromus albicollis* is placed from the south of the United States as far as the north of Argentina. Those of its sub-species which nest in the north migrate in winter; while those of warm regions stay where they are. This exemplifies why, before one can say that any given bird is a migrator, one needs to know the habits and geographical location of all the members of its family. Essentially, South American nightjars include the genera *Uropsalis*, *Macropsalis*, *Hydropsalis* and *Eleothreptus*, and a large number of species. The scissor-beaked, forked-tailed, black-and-white and lyre nightjars represent, respectively, each of these four genera.

Hummingbirds

Hummingbirds (p. 1268) feed on nectar and are fascinating to observe, as they can hover by the flowers that they feed from–moving their tiny wings so rapidly that one can barely see them. There are more than 300 species of hummingbird in the New World, all of which have a similar life-style, which results in a homogenous family, and the physical differences between the species are mainly to do with their beaks–which have adapted to the different types of flowers from which they draw their food. Hummingbirds play an important role in pollination.

Members of the family Trochilidae, hummingbirds can be found from the Alaskan mountains all the way to Cape Horn. They are distributed throughout South America (with the exception of the extreme southeast) and in North America inhabit two great regions in particular. One is all along the Pacific coast, including the Rockies, and all of Central America; the other starts north of the Great Lakes and goes down as far as the Gulf of Mexico.

Among the northern species, the ruby-throated hummingbird *Archilochus colubris* nests in the east of the United States–from the Great Lakes to the Mississippi Delta– and winters in Central America; while the rufous hummingbird *Selasphorus rufus* nests on the North Pacific coast and migrates to Mexico. The three-coloured hummingbird *S. platycercus*, on the other hand, lives in mid-North America.

Swifts (p. 2456) are cosmopolitan birds and, with hummingbirds, form the order Apodiformes. The chimney swift *Chaetura pelagica* migrates from the North American east to the Amazon, passing through Central America. No swifts are found very far north (though some species nest in northern temperate regions). Fast and strong fliers, they all migrate towards the tropics for the winter.

The Mississippi Delta

Before considering the animals that live there, it is worth taking a look at certain well-defined regions; especially as they contain species unlike those found anywhere else on the continent.

The low valley of the Mississippi forms a special region. The Mississippi Delta alone covers an area of nearly 29 000 square miles (and is disappearing into the sea at the rate of 300 ft per year). All told, the fenlands of the Mississippi occupy an area of nearly 4000 square miles and have their own particular kind of vegetation. (Similar marshes also intermittently border the low coasts of Texas as far as the Rio Grande.)

Situated to the north of the Gulf of Mexico, the Mississippi Delta is spared the violent hurricanes which affect similar regions. Its climate is tropical—hot and humid—and nothing exemplifies this better than the fact that the region has alligators. Unlike African crocodiles, the common American alligator *Alligator mississippiensis* (p. 67) lacks ossified ventral scales; its jaws and teeth are also different.

Turtles

Marsh turtles are highly representative of this region. The diamond-backed terrapin *Malaclemys terrapin* (p. 2507) is the most coastal of them, but is really a true marsh creature as it cannot stand fresh water and will only go in the sea to reach another lagoon. Interestingly, one of its enemies is another turtle: the alligator snapping turtle *Macrochelys temminckii* (p. 2303).

The musk turtles *Sternotherus odoratus* and *S. carinatus* (p. 1673) secrete an abominable odour through their anal gland—hence their alternative name of 'stinkpots'. The former is distributed throughout the south-east. The mud turtles *Kinosternon subrubrum* and *K. baurii* (p. 1673) are less well known, and the snapping turtle *Chelydra serpentina* (p. 2303), which has an interesting pattern of distribution, is famous for its aggressiveness, biting at enemies and prey with vice-like jaws.

There are seven species of terrapins of the genus *Malaclemys* which can be found in the Missisipi Delta. Well adapted, these creatures have a special gland near their eyes which eliminates surplus salt. In general, a large number of species and sub-species of turtles, terrapins and tortoises are found in North America. In the Great Lakes region there are Blanding's turtle *Emydoidea blandingii* and the painted turtle *Chrysemys picta* (p. 1814); to the east, the *Clemys guttata* and *C. insculpta*. Muhlenberg's tortoise *C. muhlenbergii* should also be pointed out.

Snakes

King snakes (p. 1367) of the genus *Lampropeltis*, including the smaller milk snakes, are very much creatures of the Mississippi Delta lands. The local common king snake *L. gutulus* will attack and kill other poisonous snakes as well as rodents, other mammals, lizards and frogs. But, in general, many snakes are found here which are related to others in different habitats across the continent. The water mocassin *Agkistrodon piscivorus*, for instance, is well and truly a marsh creature; while the copper-headed mocassin *A. contortrix* is more a forest one.

The Everglades

The Florida Everglades are a vast labyrinth of fens. They have a tropical, humid climate and luxuriant vegetation. In terms of fauna they contain many of the species we have already mentioned in reference to the Mississippi Delta—as do other marshes of the Gulf of Mexico.

Like all fenlands, the Everglades are an intermediary form of environment, half way between the land and the sea—and the animal life here reflects that. Some creatures, therefore, live permanently in the region. Others penetrate it occasionally. Birds provide an excellent example—and the Everglades are famous for them. Here, among many others, one can see: the brown pelican *Pelicanus occidentalis* (p. 1864) conscientiously fishing; the exclusively New World roseate spoonbill *Ajaia ajaja* (p. 2358); the common pink flamingo *Phoenicopterus ruber*; and a winter visitor, the crested kingfisher

Death valley in eastern California links the Great Basin desert with the Mojave desert. The hottest temperature in North America, 56.5 °C/134 °F, has been recorded here. And yet 600 species of plants, over 100 species of birds and nearly 40 species of mammals have been seen.

Megaceryle alcyon, which comes to take advantage of the region's wealth of food.

A continent of contrasts
The 100° meridian effectively divides America into two. To the east of this line there is a reasonable abundance of rain coming from the Atlantic. To the west rainfall diminishes so that, by the time one has reached the high plateaus of the west, cultivation is impossible without irrigation. Going west from the Atlantic, forest becomes more open and gives way to steppe on the plateaus. Then, from the first foot-hills of the Rockies on, an arid region begins, stretching through the Great Colorado Basin, and consisting of desert and desert steppe.

The North American desert
Desert does not necessarily imply endless sand such as one sees in the Sahara. And the word legitimately applies to any region—like the great Nevada Basin—which has no natural water.

The North American desert divides effectively into two regions: one around the Gulf of California, the other going in stages from the plateaus of Santa Fe as far as the north of Mexico—where the surrounding mountains are also low and semi-arid.

Rodents are found in all deserts. And many of them can go without drinking, provided they have certain fruits, bulbs or plants from which they can draw their water.

The North American deserts have their birds as well. The elf owl nests in tall cacti using deserted woodpecker nesting holes. The raven (p. 2051) has entered, and adapted itself to, desert and feeds on carrion there. The cactus wren *Campylorhinchus brunneicapillus* (p. 2770) lives on insects which it finds under stones; the California quail *Lophortyx californica* (p. 2002) lives on leaves and the sap of certain cacti. The nightjar has species which are adapted to the desert, too, and there are even hummingbirds there—as represented by the species *Basilinna xantusi*, *Coeligena clemenciae* and *c. uranomitra*.

Strange desert animals
Spiny lizards of the genus *Sceloporus* not only stand up to, but actively need, heat. *Sceloporus magister*, for instance, cannot digest its food effectively if the temperature falls below 37°C/98°F. The fringed-toed tree lizard *Uta ornata*, which is found in Arizona, can tolerate extraordinary temperatures.

There are seven different species of horned toad (genus *Phrynosoma*, see p. 1240)—not amphibians but a most unusual form of iguana. They are not all desert animals, but those that have adapted to the driest of regions, where they bury themselves in the sand and feed on ants. The iguanid *Uma stansburiana* of the American west ranges from regions of scanty vegetation to really arid ones with virtually none. While the lizard *Petrosaurus mearnsi* of South California is an

excellent climber, scaling sheer walls of rock.

Desert iguana (p. 1296) and chuckwalla (p. 570) belong to the genera *Dipsosaurus* and *Sauromalus* respectively. They live perfectly happily in the driest of regions and can tolerate temperatures of as much as 47°C/116°F. The North American desert iguana *D. dorsalis* functions equally well on sandy, rocky or clay soil—all in regions where there is very little to drink. The chuckwalla *S. obesus* has wrinkled skin and can be seen sunning itself on rocks. If it has to move, though, it does so with disconcerting rapidity, half drawing itself up on its hind legs—and using its supple tail as a pivot when it wants to alter direction.

The gila monster merits a paragraph on its own. It is a highly poisonous creature, and, though its bite may not be absolutely fatal for man, this is not something one would want to put to the test. There are two species, *Heloderma suspectum* and the *H. horridum*, of which the latter probably most deserves the title of monster. Some naturalists, however, say quite the reverse and give *H. horridum* the common name of beaded lizard. In any event, the gila monster is thought to be able to go without food for months. It grows to a length of 23 in.—a considerable size.

The red diamond-back rattlesnake *Crotalus ruber* (p. 2048) is even bigger and can easily grow to 6 ft long. It has obvious markings and tends to slacken itself before it strikes,

The western diamond back rattlesnake Crotalus atrox *is one of the most dangerous snakes in the world as its powerful venom can be fatal. An adult grows to 50–60 in. long.*

Albert Visage – Jacana

which it does without fully extending its body. Rattlesnakes have a great number of species in very different regions. There is a western diamond-back *C. atrox* and an eastern diamond-back *C. adamanteus*. The diamond-back is also found in Florida, where it lives alongside the timber rattler *C. horridus*. Two other rattlesnakes relevant to this region are the western diamond-back and the prairie rattlesnake *C. viridis* which can be found up to the Sierra Nevada. The little horned, or desert, rattlesnake *C. cerastes* is relatively small at around 27 in. long and lives in the steppes and deserts of the south-western United States. All these snakes have rattles at the end of their tails, which they shake in warning before they strike.

Other desert animals are the fox *Vulpes macrotis* and the desert rat, shrew-mouse and hare with a host of other tiny creatures.

Finally, it is worth mentioning that deserts can be exploited and need not remain barren. Imperial Valley—created with the help of water piped in from the Colorado River—is a good example. On the subject of water, we would like to end this section with a final word on the Great Lakes. Forming part of the frontier between the United States and Canada, these lakes constitute the largest supply of fresh water in the world. Here are found the same families of fish as in European fresh water. (All told there are 600 species of fish in North America, of which the Mississippi Basin alone has 260.)

Eric Hosking

△ *The timber or banded rattlesnake* Crotalus horridus *is found in the eastern United States.*

▽ *The Gila monster* Heloderma horridum *one of only two poisonous lizards. It lives in the deserts of south-western U.S.*

Zanin-Vendal – Jacana

American robin

The early colonists in America gave the name robin to a redbreasted bird that reminded them of the 'robin redbreast' of their homeland. Both American and European robins are members of the thrush family, as is betrayed by the speckled breast of the young birds, but the American robin is more closely related to the song thrush, blackbird and fieldfare than to the European robin. Indeed, the American robin was called the fieldfare by some colonists.

The American robin is the size of a blackbird. The head, back, wings and tail are a brown-grey, the tail being darker and the head dark brown to black, with black and white speckled throat and a white ring around the eyes. The breast and belly are brick-red, much darker than the breast of the European robin.

Van Riper

American robins have 2 or 3 broods a year and feed their nestlings on insects. Building the bowl-shaped nest may be done in one day's feverish activity by the female, the male helping only by collecting material to give to her, and if she is too busy to take it he may even drop it all

Distribution and habits

The range of the American robin covers most of the USA, as well as southern Canada. To the north, it is found breeding just beyond the tree-line, and in the south-eastern states its range is extending south-wards towards the Gulf of Mexico and the Atlantic Ocean. While the robin is more common in deciduous woodland, it is tolerant of extremes and may be found anywhere from dense forests to open plains.

The American robin is migratory, the whole population shifting south in the autumn so that the most northerly robins spend the winter where their more southerly neighbours breed. In the spring, the robins are among the first migrants to return to any area so that they are well-known as harbingers of spring, like cuckoos or swallows in England.

Although mainly a woodland bird, the American robin has achieved the same status as best-known and best-liked of wild birds as the European robin has this side of the Atlantic, because it has adapted its habits to share man's environment. They are both commonly seen searching for food on lawns and they also nest in houses and sheds, even in odd places like motor tractors.

Feeding

American robins feed on a mixture of berries and insects, no doubt turning to which-ever is most readily accessible. An exam-ination of some stomach contents showed that 42% of the diet was made up of insects; half being beetles and half grasshoppers.

Hen bird works hardest

Throughout its range the American robin is one of the first birds to begin laying. Nests are found 2–10 ft from the ground, but they may be as much as 80 ft up in trees.

Normally there are two broods; some-times three. The nest for the first is usually made in coniferous trees as the deciduous trees preferred for the second brood are bare at this time.

The nest is built by the female, with the male assisting only by collecting material. Even so, he makes fewer trips and carries less material in any trip than his industrious mate, and if she is busy shaping the nest when he arrives, he is likely to drop the lot rather than wait to give it to her.

Building the bowl-shaped nest may take as little as one day's feverish activity by the female robin. There are three stages in its construction. First the rough, outer foundations are laid down, long coarse grass, twigs, paper and feathers being woven into a cup-shaped mass. Then the bowl itself is made out of mud laid inside the main mass. If there is no readily available source of mud the robin makes her own, either by soaking a beakful of dry earth in water, or by wetting her feathers then rubbing them in earth. If there is no hurry and no egg is imminent, work will stop for a day or two to let the mud dry. Finally a

The American robin is as popular in the United States as the European robin is on the other side of the Atlantic. It was called a robin by the early colonists because its red breast reminded them of the familiar bird from 'home'. It, too, likes to live with men, searching for food on lawns and nesting in garden sheds and odd places like motor tractors. The other bird in the picture is a female Lapland Bunting or Longspur.

lining of soft grass is added.

One to six, but usually three or four, blue-green eggs are laid and are incubated for a fortnight by the female only. She continues brooding the chicks while they are very young. Later she does so only during bad weather and at night. Sometimes her mate helps feed the chicks.

Enemies

At one time the American robin was recognised as a game bird in some of the southern States. Although unlikely to have provided much sport it was no doubt as palatable as our blackbird, which once was regarded as a delicacy. Now, the robin enjoys protection over its whole range.

Cowbirds frequently parasitize American robins, laying their eggs in robins' nests in the same manner as cuckoos. Domestic cats catch adults and young, and the introduced house-sparrows, or English sparrows as they are known in America, plunder the nests.

An international feathered friend

A well-known journalist once wrote an article explaining that the friendliness of the robin redbreast was due to the bird's habit of following large animals around to feed on worms and insect grubs exposed in the earth churned up by their hoots. For the next week he was inundated with letters from readers. Some were written more in sorrow than in anger, others were plainly abusive. The best letter, signed 'Jobbing gardener, aged 65' told, in almost poetic terms, of a robin that daily shared the gardener's midday meal, and ended with the words '. . . and you can jump into a lake'.

Something of this widespread affection for the robin must have possessed the people of Great Britain from very early times for wherever they went in the world any bird with a red breast was likely to be called a robin. The most famous is the American robin, which is really a thrush, and that is why it is given this separate entry. In Australia several birds are called robins. They are mainly flycatchers. One of the same kind in New Zealand, with a red breast, is named 'robin'. There is an Indian robin, and the Peking robin commonly kept as an aviary bird, is a babbler. The Jamaican tody is called 'robin', and in various places there are robin chats, bush robins, scrub robins and magpie robins. These represent a diversity of birds, having little more in common than red feathers somewhere on the breast, that probably originally reminded settlers of home.

class	**Aves**
order	**Passeriformes**
family	**Muscicapidae**
genus & species	***Turdus migratorius***

America, South

After the break-up of Gondwanaland, South America was geographically isolated from the rest of the world for a very long time. As a result many highly original life forms evolved there. Its flora and fauna need to be looked at with this in mind; but also in relation to North America—and. Africa, to which Brazil remained joined until the early Cretaceous period.

Savannas

There are several types of savanna. Bare savanna with grassy vegetation and few trees (or none at all) is one. The savanna of Africa, the 'campo limpo' of the plateaus of Brazil, or the 'chapadoes' as they are known in the Mato Grosso, are all bare savanna.

Bordering this, one finds arboreal savanna, with a larger number of trees, but still a rich growth of grass. This is the 'campo sujo' or 'campo cerrado', in Brazil, and it.corresponds to the savanna-parklands of West Africa. Its trees are dome-shaped, and the word 'cerrado' refers to this, although it literally means scrub and is also applied to regions of dense forest.

Outside Brazil, 'campo cerrado' and 'campo sujo' become 'llanos'—which is comparable to regions of Guinea and the Sudan. The 'pampas' of the Argentine refers to the great flat surfaces of regions neighbouring the River Plate. And thorny bush is known as 'caatinga'.

Animals of the savannas

There is a wealth of creatures to be found on the various savannas of South America. A brief glance at its carnivores shows: the maned wolf *Chrysocyon brachyurus* (p. 1534) of the pampas, the ocelot *Leopardus pardalis* (p. 1742), the pampas fox *Dusicyon gymnocercus*, the Magellan or Colpeo fox *D. culpaeus* , the Azara fox *D. azarae* (p. 1742), and the Brazil hoary fox *Lycalopex vetulus*, which is a noteworthy inhabitant of the 'campos' of Brazil.

Ungulates are very well represented too (see p. 2328), due to the large expanses of grassland. Species include swamp deer *Blastocerus dichotomus*, Virginia deer *Odocoileus virginianus* (p. 1674), guemals *Hippocamelus* spp, pampas deer *Ozotoceros bezoarticus* and small brocket deer *Mazama* spp. The cottontail rabbits of the genus *Sylvilagus* (p. 671) are also well distributed in South America.

The jaguar *Panthera onca* (p. 1315) appears in slightly more humid regions. So do rodents, such as porcupines (p. 2567) and the paca *Cuniculus paca* (p. 1802)—while the edentates feature the giant ant-eater *Myrmecophaga tridactyla* (p. 161) and armadillos (p. 176) of the genera *Euphractes* and *Dasypus*. In the pampas one can sometimes find the Patagonian hare *Dolichotis patagona* (p. 1126), but the plains viscacha *Lagostomus maximus* (p. 2640), which is a member of the same family as chinchilla, is the true pampas 'hare', although it is actually a rodent.

Guinea pigs or cavies represent a phylogenetic unity peculiar to the New World, found principally from Central America on through all South America.

There are 14 genera of uniquely South American marsupials (counting the North American common or Virginian opossum) and no less than 23 sub-genera of specifically South American mosquitoes.

The South American land mass contains a vast number of birds. Two-fifths of all the world's bird species are found here, and no less than 90 families of birds are peculiar to South America alone. Birds like tyrant-flycatchers, the antbirds of the family Formicariidae and tanagers, to name but a few.

South America is also characterized by its primates, the American or New World monkeys, including the titis, uakaris, spider monkeys, woolly monkeys, tamarins and marmosets.

There are a multitude of original South American rodents, whose history dates from the Oligocene. Many first came to the continent by way of intermediary islands, where evolution also occurred in a closed environment.

Zoologists often divide South American mammals into three groups: those whose evolution occurred during its isolation; the 'island-hoppers', which arrived at different epochs via islands that appeared in the surrounding seas; and finally, all the new

After the break-up of Gondwanaland in the Cretaceous period, South America was isolated from the Palaeocene to the Pliocene epochs. This allowed the evolution of marsupials and many unique kinds of placental mammals. However, only a few of these survived the later invasion of placentals from the north.

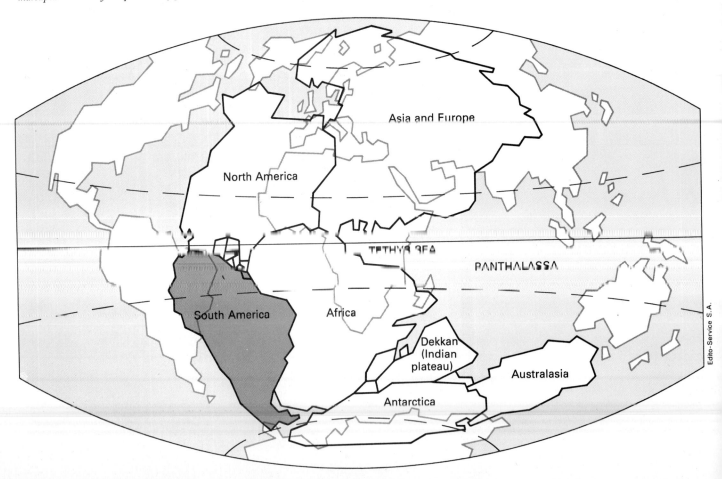

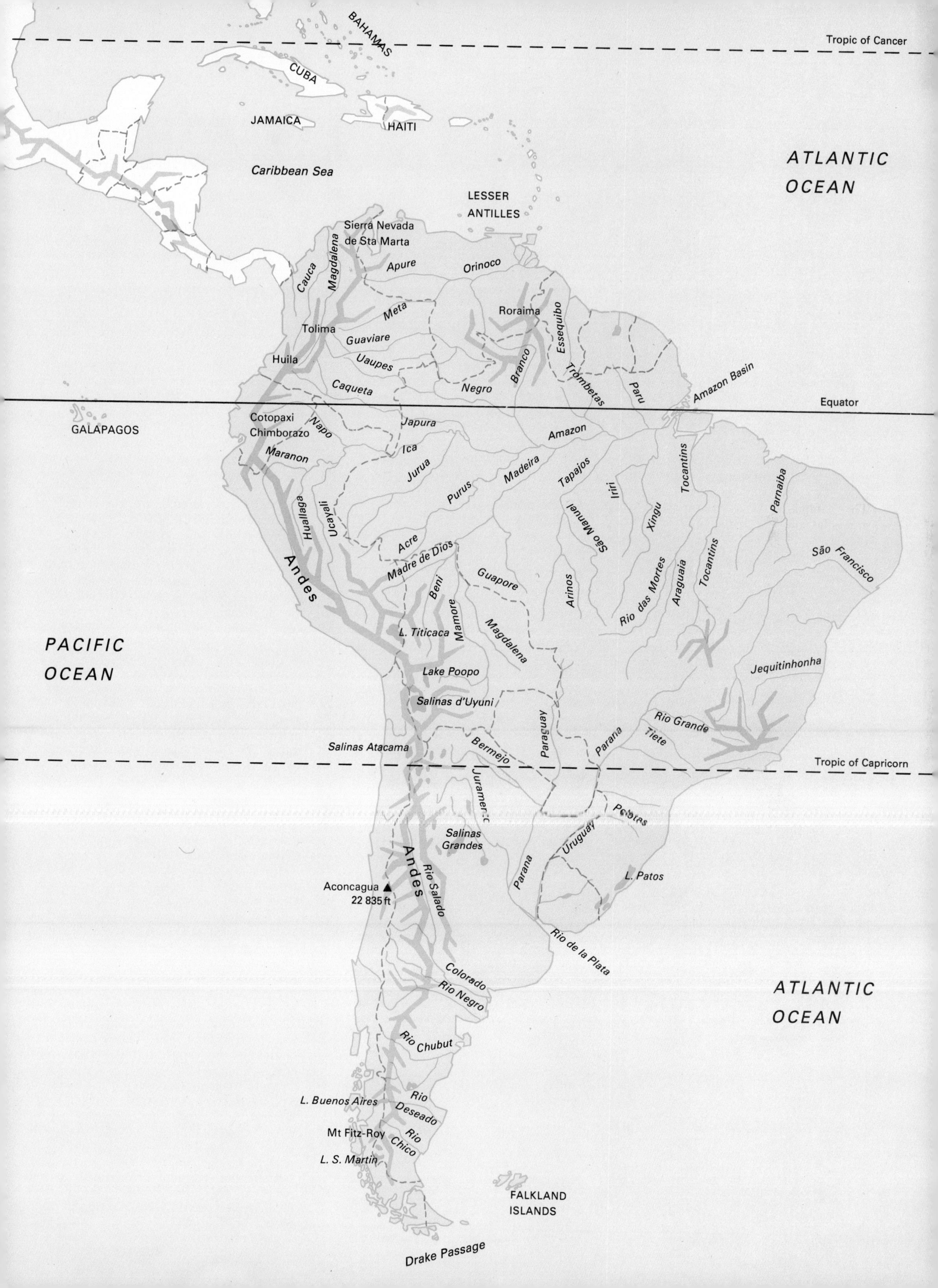

TROPIC OF CANCER *(Tropic of Cancer)*

BAHAMAS

CUBA

JAMAICA

HAITI

Caribbean Sea

LESSER
ANTILLES

ATLANTIC
OCEAN

Sierra Nevada
de Sta Marta

Magdalena

Apure

Orinoco

Cauca

Meta

Roraima

Essequibo

Tolima

Guaviare

Branco

Trombetas

Paru

Huila

Uaupes

Negro

Amazon Basin

Caqueta

Equator

GALAPAGOS

Cotopaxi
Chimborazo

Napo

Japura

Amazon

Maranon

Ica

Jurua

Madeira

Tapajos

Iriri

Xingu

Tocantins

Parnaiba

Andes

Huallaga

Ucayali

Purus

São Manuel

Araguaia

Tocantins

São Francisco

Acre

Madre de Dios

Arinos

Rio das Mortes

Beni

Guapore

PACIFIC
OCEAN

Mamore

Magdalena

Jequitinhonha

L. Titicaca

Lake Poopo

Salinas d'Uyuni

Paraguay

Parana

Rio Grande

Tiete

Salinas Atacama

Bermejo

Tropic of Capricorn

Juramen-c

Pelotas

Salinas
Grandes

Parana

Uruguay

L. Patos

Andes

Aconcagua ▲
22 835 ft

Rio Salado

Rio de la Plata

ATLANTIC
OCEAN

Colorado

Rio Negro

Rio Chubut

L. Buenos Aires

Rio
Deseado

Mt Fitz-Roy

Rio
Chico

L. S. Martin

FALKLAND
ISLANDS

Drake Passage

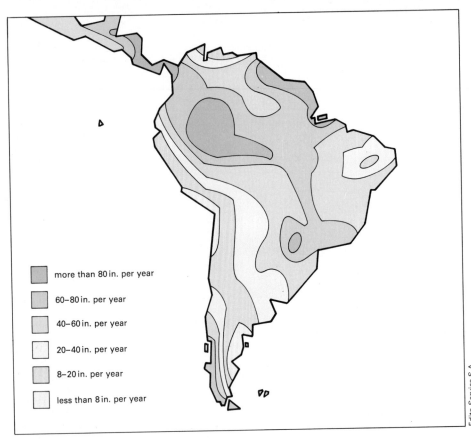

more than 80 in. per year

60–80 in. per year

40–60 in. per year

20–40 in. per year

8–20 in. per year

less than 8 in. per year

In most parts of South America, it is the trade winds coming from the Atlantic that bring the rain. Great humidity and torrid heat helps the magnificent forests to grow, particularly in the northern regions. The Pacific coast receives little rain due to the presence of the Andes. But altogether there is an incomparable variety and richness of vegetation.

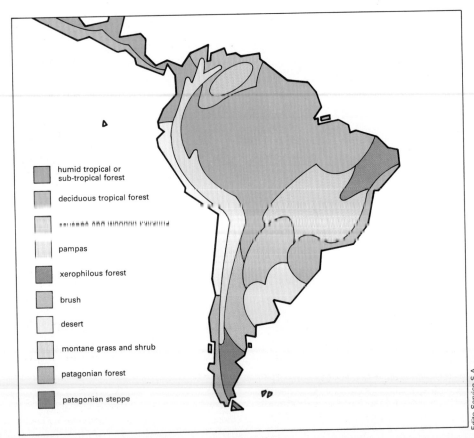

humid tropical or
sub-tropical forest

deciduous tropical forest

savanna and wooded savanna

pampas

xerophilous forest

brush

desert

montane grass and shrub

patagonian forest

patagonian steppe

species that came from the north when the continental link with North America was re-established.

Geography and topography

Like Africa, South America is a triangularly shaped land mass with a relatively unindented coastline and few islands in its immediate vicinity. To the north lie the West Indies; to the south, Tierra del Fuego—an inhospitable land that is separated from the mainland by the Magellan Straits. In the most simple terms, one could say that South America is mainly situated in a torrid climatic zone, and to a lesser extent in a southerly temperate one—but this needs qualifying.

Along the western coast of South America lie the Andes—the longest, most regular, mountain range in the world. In their middle section, they form a single range; while in the north they divide into two, then three ranges, with high plateaus between them. Over their greatest length, the Andes have an average altitude of 13 000 ft; their main peak, Aconcagua, is almost 23 000 ft high. (The Andes also enclose a large number of volcanoes.)

On its eastern side, South America has two isolated mountainous blocks—in Guyana and Brazil—consisting of plateaus and fairly low mountains. These are the apparent remainders of Pre-Cambrian formations which were subjected to a series of vertical fractures. One section of the formation, for instance, is buried under part of the Amazon basin and surfaces in Guyana. Once the western border of Gondwanaland, these formations later subsided. They nonetheless form a sub-foundation for the whole of the land mass—and they occasionally re-appear in the form of small mountains as far as Patagonia.

Between the Andes and these isolated mountains, stretch immense plains which grow lower to the east and south all the way to the Atlantic. Enormous rivers run through them. The River Orinoco waters the llanos; the River Amazon irrigates a vast region of 'selvas' (forests); the River Plate runs through the pampas, and its vast estuary is formed of the union of the River Parana and the River Uruguay.

Climate and vegetation

Trade winds off the Atlantic bring rain—and a good deal of it—to Colombia, Venezuela, Guyana and Brazil. This considerable rainfall, combined with great heat, has resulted in the tropical rain forests of the Amazon. Going south from this dense forest, one comes to savanna; prairies in the south of Brazil and Argentina, bush and steppe in Patagonia. The Pacific coast, on the other hand, receives relatively little rain—especially in Peru and the north of Chile—which has desert in the north, Mediterranean vegetation in the centre of the country, and conifers in the south.

South America is subject to what is known as an 'inter-tropical front'—which brings alternate dry and rainy seasons. Dense forest, becoming tropical rain forest with 100 in. of rain per year, covers the upper reaches of the Amazon and Orinoco and stretches both east and west towards Central America. This forest contains the greatest diversity of flora and fauna and we will come back to it.

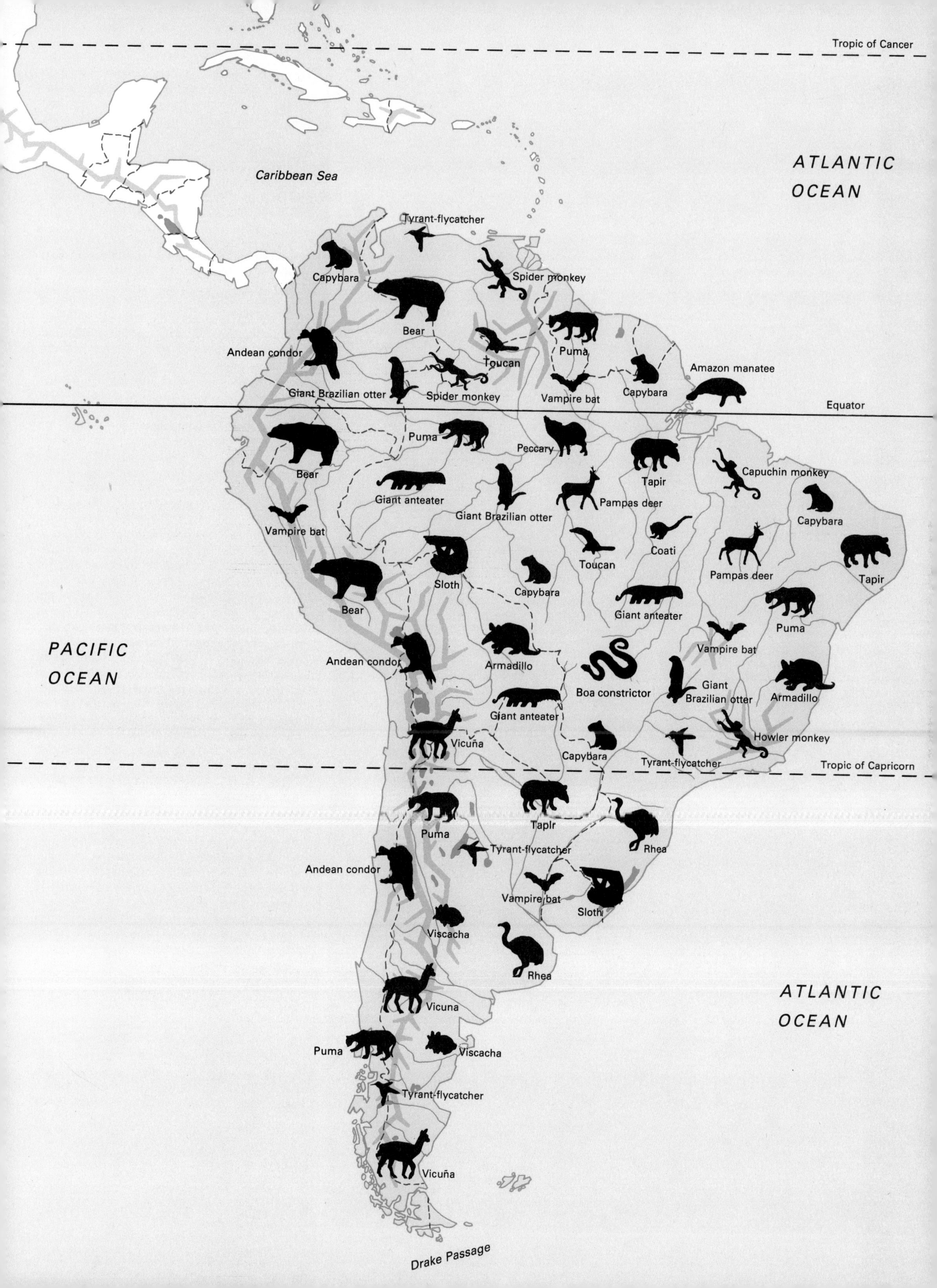

Tropic of Cancer

ATLANTIC OCEAN

Caribbean Sea

Tyrant-flycatcher

Capybara

Spider monkey

Bear

Andean condor

Puma

Toucan

Amazon manatee

Giant Brazilian otter

Spider monkey

Vampire bat

Capybara

Equator

Puma

Peccary

Bear

Capuchin monkey

Giant anteater

Tapir

Capybara

Giant Brazilian otter

Pampas deer

Vampire bat

Pampas deer

Toucan

Coati

Tapir

Sloth

Capybara

Giant anteater

Puma

PACIFIC OCEAN

Andean condor

Armadillo

Vampire bat

Boa constrictor

Giant Brazilian otter

Armadillo

Giant anteater

Howler monkey

Vicuña

Capybara

Tyrant-flycatcher

Tropic of Capricorn

Puma

Tapir

Tyrant-flycatcher

Rhea

Andean condor

Vampire bat

Sloth

ATLANTIC OCEAN

Viscacha

Rhea

Vicuna

Puma

Viscacha

Tyrant-flycatcher

Vicuña

Drake Passage

A view of the Andes from Peru.

South America's temperate zone, in the region of the River Plate, has an oceanic climate—mild winters and quite cool summers. But on the Pacific coast, maritime anticyclones and cold oceanic currents exert a disturbing influence from the Gulf of Guayaquil as far as the south. To try to divide South America into neat climatic zones is, in fact, impossible. There is desert in Chile at the same latitude as that of São Paulo on the Atlantic coast, where the climate is more or less Mediterranean.

The South American mountains and their animals

The llama (p. 1458), an artiodactyl of the camel family, exists only in the domesticated form these days, but it has played as important a role in the mountains of South America as its Old World relative, the Arabian camel, has done in the deserts and plains of North Africa. Two other animals of the same genus are the alpaca and the guanaco. The alpaca *Lama glama pacos* is slighter than the llama and is distinguished from it and the guanaco by the length of its fur. The guanaco *L. guanicoe* lives in the mountains of Chile, Peru and Ecuador. The vicuna *Vicugna vicugna* is a smaller member of the same family which is found very high in the Andes, up to 16 500 ft.

The South American mountains also harbour the pudu (p. 2328), a member of the deer family with a rounded back and slender legs. There are two species of the genus *Pudu*. One, *P. mephistopheles*, lives in Ecuador and Colombia; the other *P. pudu*, in southern Chile. The Andean deer *Hippocamelus antisiensis* of Ecuador and Peru, with their Chilean relation *H. bisulcus*, live in high mountains at altitudes of between 10 000 and 13 000 ft. The pygmy brocket deer *Mazama nana* inhabits mountain forests. The dwarf grey brocket *M. bricenii*, about which little is known, also lives at 10 000 ft. Brockets of other species and sub-species can be found in a variety of habitats.

Mountains also provide a habitat for some species one might not expect to see there—the South American mountain tapir *Tapirus pinchaque* (p. 2478), for instance. The smallest of its genus, this tapir has woolly fur and lives in the high Andes of Ecuador and Colombia. Baird's tapir *T. bairdi*, on the other hand, lives in Central America, while the Brazilian tapir is Amazonian.

Mountain carnivores which are well worth noting are: the puma *Felis concolor* (p. 2009), the pampas cat *Lynchailurus pajeros* and the Andean or mountain cat *Oreailurus jacobita*, which in general favours high plateaus more than mountains. The Magellan wolf, or fox, (*Dusicyon* spp) has a wide domain, which extends from the desert mountains of Tierra del Fuego all along the Andes as far as Ecuador. Other mountain creatures include: the Andes skunk *Conepatus rex*, found on the high plateaus of Bolivia, Peru and Chile, a representative of the family Procyonidae;

and the coati *Nasua nasua* (p. 592), a small, carnivorous mammal, which can be found in localized mountain forests.

Cavy-type rodents include mountainous animals like the mountain paca *Cuniculus taczanowskii* (p. 1802), the mountain viscacha *Lagidium peruanum* (p. 2640) and the chinchilla *Chinchilla laniger* (p. 562). The mountain paca differs from the plains species, *C. paca*, in that it is smaller and has thicker fur characteristic of the Andes. So too does the woolly chinchilla, and this is most likely due more to climatic adaptation than any fundamental difference in species.

The Andes would be unimaginable without their condors, which are integrally associated with them. The Andes condor *Vultur gryphus* (p. 644) is one of the largest birds capable of flight and has a 10 ft wingspan. It is distributed throughout the Cordilleras from Venezuela to Patagonia, though it is now extremely rare due to persecution by man. Another reason for this is the species' slow rate of reproduction, for the condor only reaches sexual maturity at the age of seven. Then, at best, each pair only produces one offspring every two years.

The seed-snipes (p. 2214) are very much smaller birds but are also found at altitude. Members of the family Thinocoridae, they look like a cross between a small quail and a plover. They live on the Pacific side of the continent, mainly on the high plateaus of the Andes. The two genera, *Thinocorus* and *Attagis*, are worth noting. The white-bellied seed-snipe *A. malouinus* is found in Ecuador, Peru and Tierra del Fuego, whereas Swainson's seed-snipe is located in the deserts of Chile.

The Rheidae is an important family, containing the two large flightless running ratites, the rheas (p. 2080). Two species exist, the common rhea or 'Nandu' of the grasslands and the Darwin's rhea that lives on the high plateaus of the Andes. The sub-species *Pterocnemia pennata galeppi* lives up to heights of 13 000 ft. Two other special birds worth noting are: the grebe of Lake Titicaca (which lies at an altitude of 10 443 ft); and the equally localized grebe of Lake Atilan on the high (11 500 ft) volcanic plateau of Guatemala.

Hummingbirds are experts at adaptation and they have one rare species that lives at altitude. This is the rachet-tailed hummingbird *Loddigesia mirabilis* (p. 1268), which is a lovely looking bird with a double spatulate tail.

Opossums

The family Didelphidae (p. 1755) numbers some 60 species peculiar to Central and South America—and only one, the Virginia opossum *Didelphis marsupialis* has ever migrated through Central America to North America, where it is very successful. Opossums range from the size of a mouse to that of an average domestic cat. They have a large number of sub-species (woolly opos-

Different members of the genus Lama. *They are generally used as beasts of burden, but the alpaca is bred for its fine wool.*

At 5 ft high, the flightless rheas are the largest of the American birds.

sums of the genus *Caluromys* alone have 20). Unlike many marsupials of Australasia, all American opossums survive extremely well.

There are ten species of murine opossums (*Monodelphis* spp). Their total length varies between 3 in. and 6 in.—and they lack the characteristic marsupial pouch. There are only two brush-tailed opossums (*Glironia* spp); but the mouse opossum (*Marmosa* spp) has around 50 species and numerous subspecies. The genera *Metachirops* and *Metachirus* are known respectively as four-eyed and rat-tailed opossums. The thick-tailed opossums of the genus *Lutreolina* grow to 12 in. and carry a reserve of fat in their very thick tails. Yapoks (*Chironectes* spp) are adapted to water and are distinguishable by their flattened tail; and finally there is the Azara's opossum *Didelphis azarae* of Paraguay and southern America.

The tropical forest

The tropical forest is a world of its own—amazingly dense, humid, hot and alive. Entering it, one of the first sounds one might hear is the strange cry of the howler monkey.

But before looking at these animals in more detail, two distinctions should be noted. All monkeys with prehensile tails live in America, and the monkeys of the Old and New Worlds are separated into two distinct groups: the catarrhines of the Old World (nostrils set close together and open to the

The Virginia opossum is widespread in North America as well as being fairly common in South America.

front) and the platyrrhines (nostrils widely separated and open to the sides) of the New World.

Monkeys

The ancestors of the platyrrhines were separated from other simians at the moment when South America became really insular. As a result, their contemporary representatives are in some ways more primitive than the catarrhines. They lack, for instance, an opposable thumb (which makes gripping easier) and, with the exception of the capuchins, their brains are less well formed.

The Cebidae form a great family which encompasses five sub-families: Aotinae, Pithecinae, Cebinae, Alouattinae and Atelinae. Then come two other families, the Callimiconidae, represented by Goeldi's monkey *Callimico goeldii*, and the Callithricidae, the marmosets and tamarins.

The sub-family Aotinae includes the night or owl monkey, also called the douroucouli *Aotus trivirgatus* (p. 799). This unique, truly nocturnal monkey is also considered to be the most primitive. It is found in humid and dry forests.

In the sub-family Pithecinae we have the sakis, the uakaris, the squirrel monkeys and capuchins. The sub-family Atelinae includes the woolly monkeys and the howler monkeys which defend their territory vocally, their ringing cries giving them their name.

The Andean condor Vultur gryphus *is one of the largest flying birds in the world.*

The white-faced saki Pithecia pithecia, *like all New World monkeys, has a broad nose with the nostrils pointing sideways.*

The red uakari is one of the two types of bald uakaris Cacajao calvus. *The face turns pale if the animal is kept out of the sunlight. It has a very limited range between two tributaries of the River Amazon, the Japurá and the Içá.*

Titis

It is hard to know quite where the titi monkeys (p. 2538) of the virgin forest are distributed, as this region is far from fully explored yet. The masked titi *Callicebus personatus* is geographically detached on the Atlantic coast and 24 sub-species of them have been counted – not an easy task as, within the same species, coloration varies according to region. In the Amazon jungle we find the collared titi *C. torquatus*, the red titi *C. cupreus*, and the orabassu titi *C. moloch*. All these titis are superb jumpers and feed as happily on insects, lizards and birds as they do on fruit and other kinds of vegetation. Titis have a cry that rivals that of howler monkeys. They move more slowly than most New World monkeys.

Saki and uakari monkeys

Sakis (p. 2131) and uakaris (p. 2619) resemble each other. The lesser saki has a very long coat and a long and bushy tail. It includes species whose names describe them well. The hairy saki *Pithecia monacha*, for example, has a toupee-like tuft of hair on its head which looks as if it is growing from a shrunken head. The pale-headed saki *P. pithecia* has two main sub-species – the white-headed saki and the golden-headed. The bearded sakis (*Chiropotes* spp) have very long head hair. They include the black saki *C. satanas*, the monk saki *C. chiropotes* and the white-nosed saki *C. albinasus*.

The naked-headed uakaris (*Cacajao* spp) are represented by four species, the bald uakari *C. calvus*, the red uakari *C. rubicundus* (which has a red face), the black-headed *C. melanocephalus* (which has a black face), and Roosevelt's uakari *C. roosevelti* (which is distinguished by its slightly greater size and relatively long tail)

Capuchins and squirrel monkeys

The members of the sub-family Cebinae are classed in two groups: the squirrel monkeys (p. 2376) and the capuchins (p. 502) – which are the most intelligent New World monkeys of all. The squirrel monkeys divide into numerous regional forms, but the principal species include the yellow or common squirrel monkey *Saimiri sciureus*, the red-back squirrel monkey *S. oerstedi*, the black-headed squirrel monkey *S. boliviensis* and the Madeira squirrel monkey *S. madeira*. The

The common marmoset Callithrix jacchus. *Marmosets are very active monkeys and they live in the upper canopy of the trees.*

capuchins consist of the monk or white-throated capuchin *Cebus capucinus*, the white-fronted capuchin *C. albifrons*, the weeper capuchin *C. negrivittatus*, and the brown capuchin *C. apella*.

All capuchin monkeys are essentially arboreal and squirrel monkeys will only come to the ground if forced to. These monkeys live at the top of the tallest trees in a canopy of verdure. The capuchins are well distributed in all the humid forests of the south—though they can also be found at altitudes of more than 5000 ft in mountainous woods very close to the Andes. They like the thickest forests, but sometimes will seek food in regions inhabited by man. As a general rule they only come down from their trees to drink.

Howlers and woolly monkeys

Howlers, woolly and spider monkeys all have what one might call a fifth hand—their prehensile tail, and they can use it most effectively to grasp, climb or hang. The largest of American monkeys, howlers (p. 1266) have a wide distribution which is compartmentalized in families. The mantled howler *Alouatta palliata* and rufous-handed howler *A. belzebul* live deep in the Amazon; the black howler *A. caraya* on the Atlantic coast; and the Guatemala howler *A. villosa*, red howler *A. seniculus* and brown howler *A. fusca* are found between them. It is not known for certain whether they howl to broadcast territorial claims or merely out of exuberance. Probably the answer is that they do it for both reasons.

Woolly monkeys (p. 2763) live in rain forest, but are also found in the region of the Andes—in which case their fur becomes longer and of a more sombre colour. Woolly monkeys can even be found in swampy forests as well. Their appearance varies according to their habitat. They move through the forest with singular ease (though they cannot rival spider monkeys which are extremely agile). Woolly monkeys worth noting include Humboldt's woolly monkey *Lagothrix lagothrica*, the smoky woolly monkey *L. cana* and Hendee's woolly monkey *L. hendeei*.

Spider monkeys (p. 2348) include the black-handed or Central American spider monkey *Ateles geoffroyi*, the brown-headed spider monkey *A. fusciceps*, the long-haired

spider monkey *A. belzebuth* and the black spider monkey *A. paniscus*. All of these monkeys have the ability to cling to almost anything, and jump magnificently. The woolly spider monkey *Brachyteles arachnoides* is the rarest of them all.

Marmosets

Goeldi's marmoset *Callimico goeldii* lives in the upper Amazon and marmosets of the genus *Callithrix* (p. 1557) are found here as well. Distributed in groups of small-sized species, they move rather like squirrels and only use their tails to balance with. Their hands, though, are grasping, and, rather than nails, their fingers have claws which make them excellent climbers. They also, uniquely, have tactile hairs on their wrists, which may help them to climb as well. The smallest marmoset, the delicate *Callithrix pygmea*, has a body only 6 in. long, and an equally long tail. It weighs less than 3½ oz and lives in Peru.

Tufted marmosets are found in Brazil. The common marmoset *Callithrix jacchus*, which has a white tuft, lives in the east and the buff-headed marmoset *C. flaviceps* lives in the centre. The brushed or white-eared marmoset *C. aurita* lives in the coastal mountains of south Brazil.

In general, young marmosets have different coloured fur to that of the adult (theirs being basically brown with yellow tips). But sub-species of marmosets can have different coloration and some pale breeds have undergone a different evolution to that of other groups. The black-pencilled marmoset *C. pencillata* lives in the plains; the white-headed *C. leucocephala* inhabits the forest regions of Minas Gerais and the coastal region of Espirito Santo. The caped marmoset *C. humeralifer* is found in Bahia, near the bay, and the white-collared marmoset *C. albicollis* also lives in this region.

Returning to the interior of the continent, one comes to the yellow-legged silky marmoset *C. chrysoleucos* which is white with a yellow rump. It lives between the Madeira and Tapajoz rivers. The Santarum marmoset *C. santaremensis* can be found in almost the same region of the central Amazon.

The majority of the pale species just mentioned are of the melanuric group—whose representative type is the silvery marmoset *C. argentata*. This is another species with numerous sub-species. A black-tailed one lives in the lower Amazon basin, a white-stomached in the Mato Grosso, and a brown-pawed in the south of Paraguay.

Tamarin monkeys

Tamarins are an important group and, to distinguish between them, each species really needs to be described in close detail. To simplify this process, they can be grouped in terms of categories and some naturalists divide them simply into hairy-faced tamarins and bare-faced. They then distribute them according to these two criteria: in the hairy-faced genus *Lentocebus* they place the species:

The cottontop or Pinché tamarin Saguinus oedipus with its white crest. It lives in the upper layers of the trees in northern Colombia and Panama.

J.-P. Varin — Jacana

midas, nigricollis, fuscicollis, melanoleucus, mystax, labiatus and imperator; in the bare-faced (same genus) are found the species bicolor, oedipus, inustus and leucopus.

It is probably more satisfactory, however, to divide tamarins into three groups: golden lion-monkeys (*Leontideus*); true tamarins (*Saguinus*), with some sub-groups like the black-faced tamarin (*Saguinus midas*), the moustached tamarin (*Tamarinus*) and the bi-coloured tamarin (*Marikina*); and, finally, the genus *Oedipomidas*.

Lion-monkeys have silky golden fur and are distributed in three main species: one in the wooded region south of Rio de Janeiro; another at Bahia; the third (which is quite rare) near São Paulo. The second group of tamarins of the genus *Saguinus* is peculiar to the Amazon, while the third group, *Oedipomidas*, lives near the isthmus in Colombia.

South American snakes

Boas and pythons (family Boidae) are among the most important of all South American snakes. The best known, the common boa constrictor *Boa constrictor* (p. 386), is found from Mexico all the way to the north of Argentina. There is only one North American member of the family found in the Californian region. The rest live from Central America southwards. The pygmy python (sub-family Loxoceminae) and boas (sub-family Boinae), live in Central America. Small boas, or wood snakes, of the genus *Tropidophis* are found in the Antilles, and the genus *Trachyboa* is found in Ecuador. The genus *Epicrates* has six Antilles species and one mainland—the rainbow boa *E. cenchris*. This is a versatile reptile, quite able to catch small rodents on the ground, and equally successful at climbing trees to feed on bats.

The false coral snake *Anilius scytale* is another very widespread South American reptile and its distribution extends over Venezuela, a good part of Colombia and Peru, and almost all of Brazil. Along with the tube (or pipe) snakes found in southern Asia as well as South America, it forms part of the family Aniliidae.

The genus *Corallus* includes the boas of northern South America and Brazil. It has a large number of sub-species and the *C. enydris* alone numbers several in tropical regions. These boas are arboreal and Cook's tree boa (*C. e. cookii*) is especially agile. In mountain forest, however, boa constrictors live on the ground.

Anacondas

Anacondas must be among the most awe-inspiring sights in the animal world. For at a staggering 30 ft long, the giant anaconda *Eunectes murinus* is the largest boa and longest of all living reptiles. In general, anacondas like water, but feed on land animals. Though these are the giants of the constrictors, the yellow anaconda *E. notaeus* grows to little more than 10 ft long. Those of the genus *Drymobius* are found in the north and in Central America.

Poisonous snakes

The Boignae (a sub-family of the family Colubridae) of the New World include venomous species in Guyana and Brazil. The banded rear-fanged snake *Oxyrophus*

Hervé Chaumeton – Jacana

△ *Cook's tree boa, which resembles the dangerous fer-de-lance — an effective defence.*

▽ *The anaconda or water boa* Eunectes murinus *is the world's largest snake.*

Devez – Jacana

trigeminus has a ringed black and red body; the South American snake-eating mussurana *Clelia clelia* is 6 ft long with an entirely blue (or sometimes black with old age) body. It can take on, and even get the better of, rattlesnakes.

American members of the family Elapidae, which includes cobras and coral snakes, live in foliage, under bushes or stones, and are seldom seen. The Brazilian coral snake *Micrurus corallinus* (p. 662) is amongst the most venomous of the family; but the majority of elapids are Mexican and Central American. There are two kinds of coral snakes, the real coral snakes and the false ones, which look like them. This sort of protective mimicry is frequently found among snakes.

The pit-viper family, the Crotalidae, which include the North American rattle-snakes, are among the most poisonous of all snakes. In Central and South America the genus *Bothrops* predominates and the arboreal, infamous and deadly fer-de-lance *B. atrox* (p. 898) is widely distributed from the south of Mexico, through all Central America and down to Peru and Brazil. The jararaca, as it is known in its more southern range, is no less dangerous, and between the two, one finds the jararacussu, another local name, which lives in humid jungle.

The largest of all the crotalids is the bushmaster *Lachesis mutus* (p. 1921), which grows to 12½ ft long. Known also as the lord of the bush, it in fact lives unobtrusively in mountainous virgin forest. It is extremely powerful, venomous and silent, with ¾ in. fangs in a 6 ft specimen.

Southern iguanas
The spiny lizards of the Sceloporinae live in North America; the Tropidurinae, Iguaninae, Basiliscinae and Anolinae are located in South America. Central America has a few members of the first two sub-families.

The small land iguana *Tropidurus torquatus* belongs in the great Amazon region, though it does not go into deep forest and prefers to stay in the open. Peru and Argentina have two flat-bodied iguanas of the genera *Ctenoblepharis* and *Phrynosoma* (horned toads). Without naming all the iguanas, it is worth pointing out that there are seven species which encompass 50 different types—all of them united in the five sub-families originally mentioned.

South America, in fact, has a wealth of species of iguanids (p. 1296) and agamids (p. 59). Those of its islands include the Antilles ground iguanas (*Cyclura* spp), more primitive members of the iguana family. On the mainland, the thorny-tailed iguanas (*Urocentron* spp) are distributed throughout the Amazon Basin. Members of this species have flat tails that are shorter than their bodies.

The spiny-tailed lizard *Urocentron azureum*, an excellent climber, is green in its natural state—but turns blue in captivity. There are four species of *Urocentron*, including *U. superciliosum*, which has a crest on its back and the nape of its neck and can be seen near tropical watercourses. *Plica umbra*, a multi-coloured lizard, lives in rain forests.

There are a large number of different forms of smooth-throated lizards, *Liolaemus* spp. They are not all known, but have a wide geographical distribution. A Peruvian species, *L. multiformis*, can be found at altitudes of between 13 000 and 16 500 ft in the Andes; while *L. magellanicus* has even reached Tierra del Fuego. These iguanas are well

The three-toed sloth Bradypus tridactylus. *Nearly all of a sloth's life is spent upside-down.*

adapted to mountains, and when they live at altitude, the females of the species carry their eggs inside them up to the very moment of hatching.

The genera *Proctotrecus* and *Stenocercus* (the narrow-tailed iguanids) are distributed in distinct species. For example, *P. azureus* lives in Brazil, Uruguay and Argentina, and *P. ornatissimus* lives in Peru and Ecuador. Chile has its own sub-species. The narrow-tailed iguanids belong in Peru, and the genus *Hoplocercus* lives in the open-wooded savanna of Brazil—beneath scrub from which it only emerges at dusk.

True iguanas of the sub-family Iguaninae are principally Central American, but some have gone north, others south. The green iguana *Iguana iguana*, for instance, belongs to the latter group—and another species, the bare-necked *I. delicatissima* lives in the Caribbean.

The arboreal basilisks (p. 297), sub-family Basiliscinae, include three genera which can be met from Mexico to the equator. They are distinguished by the helmet-like hollow crests on their heads to which they owe their name *Basiliscus*. Their diet consists of fruit and small animals. There are five species, mainly identifiable through the males, which exhibit their characteristic features of crests and back frills. Basilisks are at home in the water; while helmeted iguanas, genus *Cortyophanes*, which are related to them, are decidedly arboreal. The helmeted lizard *C. cristatus* is often located in the most extraordinary situations. Other helmeted iguanas, genus *Laemanctus*, have long legs and relatively frail bodies. All basilisks are essentially Central American—and only penetrate as far as the north of South America.

The anoles (p. 138) of the sub-family Anolinae have representatives in some 20 genera. They are commonly known as chameleons, but this can be misleading, as true chameleons are found only in Africa and in Madagascar. The long-legged iguanid *Polychrus marmoratus* is found on the borders of tropical forests. It is distinguished by its very long tail, which serves to balance it. The Brazilian iguanid *Enyalius catenatus* resembles the chameleon proper. Normally brown, it turns green when agitated. *Chamaeleolis chamaeleontides* lives in Cuba. Members of the genus *Anolis* (false chameleons) are found in the Colombian Andes, where they have become acclimatized to the cold and rain. All told, there are no less than 300 different forms. Among these, *A. equestris* lives at the very tops of trees; *A. porcatus* is more generally arboreal; the prairie *A. ophiolepis* lives on the ground; *A. vermiculatus* is found close to water; and *A. lucius* lies in holes or faults in the ground—or in inextricably tangled vegetation.

The edentates

Sloths and edentates were among the first mammals of the southern continent. At the end of the Tertiary most of them travelled, in some considerable numbers, quite far into northern America. But their elaborate degree of specialization did not favour their continued existence there. Today, sloths, armadillos and anteaters are the most primitive mammals still living in the Americas.

Armadillos

Armadillos (p. 176) are the only mammals with a carapace or shell. However, it is not a shell in the strict sense of the word, as it is not one solid mass but instead composed of

The nine-banded armadillo Dasypus novemcinctus *is found in both North and South America.*

rings of epidermal bone—which are linked by flexible tissue across the armadillo's back and sides. The advantage of this arrangement is that, while it provides all the protection of a shell, the armadillo's carapace is far more flexible and allows the creature much greater freedom of movement. The number of bands of links that go to form it also provide the means by which we distinguish between armadillos—and there are those with nine, six and three bands. The latter belong to the genus *Tolypeutes*. They live on the pampas and roll themselves into a ball when threatened, which is a highly effective means of defence.

The medium-sized armadillos, genus *Dasypus*, have pectoral and convex pelvic belts, whose number of bands also varies. Kappler's armadillo *D. kappleri* is the rarest and also the largest. It is found in Guyana,

Ecuador and Peru. The nine-banded armadillo *D. novemcinctus* is the only species to have reached North America. The seven-banded armadillo *D. septemcinctus* is found in the east of Brazil. While the hairy armadillo *D. pilosus* lives at altitude in Ecuador and Peru.

The three-banded armadillo *Tolypeutes murieie* has sub-species with between two and four bands and is well distributed in Bolivia, south Brazil and Argentina. Buffon's armadillo *T. trinctus* lives more to the south. The giant armadillo *Priodontes giganteus* belongs to a species with 11 bands, and the broad-banded armadillo *Cabassous unicinctus* is designated precisely in reference to them. This latter species has the sub-species *Lugubris*, *Hispidus* and *Loricatus* distributed in different regions, from Colombia to Guyana. They are also found in Brazil, where they

vary between north and south, and finally, they are distributed in northern Argentina and the Mato Grosso.

All armadillos are burrowers, and the six-banded armadillo is really expert at it. The genus *Euphractus* has a good distribution, from Brazil to the south of the Argentine. It incorporates the six-banded armadillo *E. sexcinctus*, the hairy armadillo *E. villosus* and the little armadillo *E. pichiy*. The fairy armadillo or lesser pichichiego *Chlamydophorus truncatus* and the greater fairy armadillo *Burmeisteria retusa* are small, pink-shelled, white-haired armadillos and well deserve their 'fairy' names. They live mole-like lives. The greater fairy armadillo lacks a pectoral belt and instead it has 24 adherent bands. All armadillos are distributed according to climate and terrain and each species has its own well-defined habitat.

The giant anteater Myrmecophagus tridactyla *is found in swamps, open forests and savannas.*

The New World parakeets, ranging from Mexico to Paraguay, are related to macaws.

Sloths and anteaters

Sloths (p. 2285) are basically armadillos, without the armour. They belong to the family Bradypodidae, which is sometimes incorporated into the infra-order Pilosa (armourless edentates), which includes great anteaters and sloths. (Classification provides the order Edentata, sub-order Xenarthra, infra-order Pilosa, with seven species distributed in two genera, *Choloepus* and *Bradypus*.) Sloths spend the larger part of their lives upside down, hanging with long arms and legs from branches, with their bellies to the sky. Two-toed sloths have two digits on the fore-limbs, three on the hind limbs, while the three-toed have three on each limb. Their classification as edentates, which means toothless, is somewhat confusing as only anteaters are entirely without teeth, and sloths can really bite.

There are two species of two-toed sloth – with different numbers of cervical vertebra – Hoffman's sloth *Choloepus hoffmani* and the two-toed sloth *C. didactylus*. They are distributed from Panama to Venezuela, in Guyana, Ecuador and Bolivia, and stop at Brazil. Hoffman's sloth has an appreciably more northern distribution than the others and is also more rare.

There are three species of three-toed sloth with several sub-species. The three-toed sloth stays close to rivers and trees where leaves provide its staple diet. The three-toed sloth *Bradypus tridactylus* and the hooded sloth *B. cuculliger* extend from the Honduras to the north of Argentina. The necklaced sloth *B. torquatus* confines itself to north-western Brazil and Peru.

The family Myrmecophagidae (p. 161) consists of South American mammals known as giant anteaters, tamanduas and dwarf anteaters. They are all 'anteaters', but the term is also applied to many other animals which also feed on ants and have comparable physiological adaptations (such as echidnas, pangolins, marsupial anteaters, aardvarks and aardwolves).

The giant anteater *Myrmecophaga tridactyla* is the size of a large dog. It is exclusively terrestrial and found in open forests and bushy savanna from Costa Rica to Gran Chaco. It is also a good swimmer and can cross major watercourses. The tamandua *Tamandua tetradactyla*, which is half its size, lives in comparable regions, but is semi-arboreal. It has a thick coat and total length of slightly less than 2 ft, of which half is taken up by its tail. The dwarf anteater *Cyclopes didactylus* is the smallest of the family. The size of a squirrel, it lives at the tops of trees and can be found from Central America to Bolivia and central Brazil. Anteaters feed on termites, ants and soft grubs.

△ *Two blue and yellow macaws* Ara ararauna *engrossed in conversation.*

▽ *The toco toucan* Ramphastos toco. *The function of its large bill, which is light but very strong, is a mystery. It could be merely an ornament or signal in aggressive or courtship displays.*

Amazons and aras

Amazons (p. 1844) and aras (p. 1497) are typical birds of the South American forest, often being called macaws. Amazons are not quite as localized as their name would have one believe, and other parakeets like the Patagonia *Cyanoliseues patagonus* can be found well to the south.

The sub-family Psittacinae divides into five groups and the Psittacini group (which includes the genera *Pionus*, *Deroptyus* and *Amazona*) has a wealth of species in Africa, Madagascar – and Central and South America. Amazons alone number 26 species and 52 sub-species peculiar to the American continent. Birds of predominantly green plumage, they are differentiated by the colours on their heads or other parts of the body. None of these birds are particularly impressive fliers, but in dense forest it is far more useful to be a good climber. In general, Amazon parrots are attractive birds and their names – like yellow-headed, blue-fronted, orange-winged – evoke this.

The white-fronted parrot *Pionus senilis* is a member of the same family and lives in Central America. The mailed parrot *Deroptyus accipitrinus* is South American – as is the vulture-parrot *Gypopsitta vulturina* of Guyana.

The sparrow parrotlet *Forpus passerinus* introduces the conure family. The yellow-mirrored parakeet *Brotogeris versicolurus* lives in the east of Brazil, tovi and toui parakeets in Venezuela, Colombia and the upper Amazon Basin. All told, there are 17 kinds of conures (p. 1841). Two of them – the little aymara parakeet *Amoropsittaca aymara* and the mouse-parakeet of the genus *Myiopsitta* – are found quite far south in the Argentine.

Macaws are the largest species of parrot and live in tropical forests. They have the most strikingly coloured plumage and their feathers have long been used by the native tribes for decoration. These parrots feed on seeds and fruit and can easily crack open even the hardest casings, such as Brazil nuts, with their powerful beaks. These beaks are so large in fact that they take up almost half the birds' heads. They are also articulated and macaws will use them to climb with, and even hang from. Another interesting feature of these birds is their zygodactylus feet (with two of their toes pointing forwards, two back, as in all parrots and woodpeckers), which make climbing easier. Over short distances macaws are also strong fliers.

Macaws are distributed in two genera: *Ara* and *Anodorhynchus*. The latter numbers three species, among them the largest of the order, the hyacinth macaw *Anodorhynchus hyacinthinus*, which grows to very nearly 3 ft in size. Its face is partly covered with feathers and its overall brilliant blue plumage gives it a majestic appearance. It reigns over the Amazon region, from the mouth of the river deep into the interior.

The genus *Ara* numbers many other species and sub-species. The scarlet red macaw *A. macao* rivals the hyacinth macaw in size and is found from Mexico to Bolivia. The blue and yellow macaws (often seen in zoos) live in the wild from Panama to Argentina. Along with the scarlet macaw, the continent's most northerly ara is the brown-fronted macaw *Ara severa*. The military macaw *Ara militaris* has a distribution which extends over more than half the land.

The macaw is a privileged bird, in the sense that its size and strength protect it from birds of prey.

Toucans

There are 37 species of toucan (p. 2554), all of different sizes and all South American. Toucans are ungainly looking birds with vast beaks that seem out of all proportion to their bodies. This beak is an infallible and multi-coloured point of recognition—and toucans are sometimes called 'clown' and 'buffoon' as a result of it.

Toucanets represent smaller species with toothed beaks. Hill toucanets (*Andigena* spp), with a black beak, can be found in the Andes, the genus *Pteroglossus* on the plains, the colourful aracaris (*Pteroglossus* spp) are also members of the family. Toucans of the genus *Ramphastos*, which include the 2 ft toco toucan, are the largest and live in low, dense forest.

Tanagers are among the most colourful of South American forest birds. The three-coloured tanager *Tangara seledon* is often mentioned for its beauty. It is found from south Brazil to the north of the Argentine. Altogether, the sub-family Thraupinae is broadly distributed through its four breeds and large number of genera—which include some 200 species, almost all of them American.

Countless song birds

Seven species of woodpecker of the genus *Phlococeastes* are found from Mexico to Argentina, and the very number of South American songbirds is almost stupefying. The sub-order Mesomyodae includes two super-families. Woodcreepers, antbirds, ovenbirds, tapaculos and little cocks form the first—the Furnarioidae; while the second super-family, the Tyrannoidae, consists of pittas or jewel thrushes (p. 1919), asities or philepittas, plant-cutters and xeniques, ten sub-families of tyrant-flycatchers, sharpbills, manakins, cotingas and plant-cutters.

In the family Dendrocolaptidae there are from 50 to 60 species of woodcreepers or woodhewers (p. 2748). Ovenbirds (p. 1789) of the family Furnariidae are classed in three distinct groups containing more than 200 species. The antbirds (p. 159) of the family Formicariidae are appreciably more numerous with 226 species, and there are 28 species of tapaculos and little cocks of the family Rhinocryptidae.

Tyrant-flycatchers (p. 2618) are widespread in both Americas, though their strongest contingent is found in South America. The families mentioned represent about 365 species distributed in 115 genera. The sharpbill (*Oxyruncus cristatus*) alone represents one family, the Oxyruncidae.

Manakins (p. 1527) of the family Pipridae which has some 20 genera, have approximately 60 species. They live mainly in tropical rain forests, and their intricate nuptial display has resulted in their alternative

Manakins live in the forests of Central and South America. The males are very brightly coloured, whereas the females are usually inconspicuous.

name-dancing birds. Manakins are considered to be good-luck birds in the Amazon region.

Cotingas (p. 669) of the family Cotingidae form a heterogenous group of 30 genera, some of which are not well known. Others are quite often seen in zoo aviaries, such as the resplendent cock-of-the-rock (p. 604). Most live in the tall, full-grown trees of tropical rain forests. Among the bizarre forms are the umbrella bird, tityr, the flame-coloured cock-of-the-rock and bellbirds (p. 331).

Plant-cutters live in the south-west of the continent and have a unique speciality – they cut down plants to gather their fruit in a wasteful, parrot-like manner – and so have earned the name phytotomes. The family Phytotomidae has three species. They have short conical beaks that are edged with teeth. One species does quite a lot of damage in Chile and the Argentine, another in Uruguay and Bolivia, while the third lives in north-eastern Peru.

Other local songbirds worth mentioning briefly are mocking-birds (p. 1626) and cardinals (p. 508), American warblers with their sub-family Virgeonidae, the sugar-birds (p. 2417), and the family Icteridae, which includes the American orioles, bobolinks and grackles (p. 1076).

Tropical jungles

It is virtually impossible to see the ground in a dense tropical forest. The heat, soil and extraordinary humidity combine to produce a jungle of inextricably tangled vegetation. In some regions, in fact, rainfall is so heavy one could effectively consider their forests aquatic. Even today few men have penetrated far into the dense immensity of these jungles and little is therefore known about some of the animals that live there.

In the constant humidity of the tropical rain forest, the factors which bear upon its flora are sunlight and temperature – which alter vertically, rising from the forest floor. As a result, vegetation becomes organized into characteristic strata. There is a world of difference between the top of a 130 ft tree and the ground, and animals – particularly insects – are distributed in direct relation to the different environments provided by these various types of vegetation.

The micro-climate of the forest floor induces a superabundance of life. Microscopic animals, such as amoeba (p. 123), abound. In fact, of all mainland habitats, the litter of the tropical rain forest is the most rich in fauna. Earthworms (p. 815), woodlice (p. 2752), spiders and other arachnids, all find as much food as they could possibly need there – and here too live flatworms (p. 928),

ribbonworms, roundworms and peripatus. Peripatus (p. 1876), or velvet worms, are also interesting because they help us trace the movement of continents, being found in all tropical parts of the world that once formed Gondwanaland.

Larvae, butterflies and ants

Tropical rain forests support a considerable and varied fauna. Look at a fallen tree, already tainted with decomposition, and you will immediately see a micro-world of life, an environment that is repeated throughout the forest. The same collection of animals will be found beneath the bark of any rotting trunk.

Butterflies emerge from larvae that develop in decomposing humus. Beetles are everywhere. The beetle *Calodoma sycophanta* is a beautiful specimen with green and gold wing-sheaths. A member of the ground-beetle (family Carabidae), its larva is armoured – and predatory. Another jungle beetle, the giant capricornis, haunts the jungle of Venezuela and Guyana.

To describe a virgin forest and not mention ants would be unthinkable. Migratory army ants (p. 180) of the genus *Eciton* are peculiar to South America. These creatures build no permanent nests and only bivouac in the course of their endless march through the forest. Leaf-cutter ants (p. 1418) of the genus *Atta* specialize in cutting up leaves, and also defend themselves most effectively. Arboreal ants of the genus *Pseudomyrma* build hanging nests on the high branches of the tallest trees in Brazil and Guyana. Tropical jungles also abound in spiders – like the great trap-door spiders (p. 2557) and the eyeless *Cryptocellus*.

Curassows and other curiosities

The family Cracidae includes curassows, guans and chachalacas, which are all curious birds found exclusively in tropical and sub-tropical American forests. There are a dozen species of these birds, the family being related to gamebirds. Curassows (p. 726) of the genus *Crax* feed in trees, on fruit, nuts, buds and young leaves – though young curassows are also fond of insects. Guans of the genus *Penelope* are small, graceful members that feed in the crown of the forest. The chachalacas of the genus *Ortalis* look like small, slender female pheasants with a long and expansive tail.

The hoatzin (p. 1211) is a strange and distant descendant of birds which lived many millions of years ago. It is confined to flooded forests along the great rivers of northern South America. The entire existence of the hoatzin *Opisthocomus hoazin* is determined by its special digestive system; while, to make up for their lack of wing development, young hoatzins have two claws on each wing which are operated by special muscles.

Trumpeters of the genus *Psophia* (p. 2586) are profiteers. They follow hoatzins, parrots,

Hans Reinhard: Bruce Coleman Ltd.

A male and female crested curassow Crax alector. Curassows live in the forests of Mexico, northern Argentina and Uruguay, feeding on nuts, soft fruits and buds.

A grey brocket deer Mazama gourzouoira. *Brocket deer are the most numerous of the South American deer and are found in many parts of northern South America and in Central America. Shy, secretive animals they move about alone or in pairs.*

toucans and howler monkeys and feed on the food that is dropped down to them on the forest floor (though they are also carnivorous). There are three species of trumpeters. They fly poorly and all live in the humid, tropical Amazon jungle region. They are dark-coloured, pheasant-sized birds with long necks and legs which makes them look like small cranes.

Tapirs and deer

Forest animals that feed on leaves and the young shoots of trees, tapirs (p. 2478), such as the South American tapir *Tapirus terrestris*, can also be found in open country. Tapirs need water and swim well—watercourses are no obstacle to them; and South American tapirs can be found in quite different regions, including the South American steppes (which are often high lands).

The marsh deer *Blastocerus dichotomus* (p. 2328) lives chiefly in Paraguay and, as we have seen, Virginia or white-tailed deer *Odocoileus virginianus* (p. 1674) also occupy large areas of South America. The pampas deer *Ozotoceros bezoarticus* (p. 2328) lives on dry, open steppes, and has a sub-species in Patagonia. Guemals (*Hippocamelus* spp, p. 2328) are mountain-dwellers in Peru and Chile. Brocket deer, in particular the grey brocket *Mazama gouasoubira* (p. 2328), are divided between forests and savannas. Pygmy brocket deer have been located in mountainous regions, as have pudu deer (p. 2328)–but it is entirely possible that one or other of them has more than one habitat.

South American rodents

The origin of South American rodents is a controversial subject. But those of the most ancient origin probably reached the land by way of infiltration from island chains. These rodents are generally referred to as cavies, from which the domestic guinea pigs (p. 1126) originate, but need to be more elaborately differentiated–as each species of the sub-order Caviomorpha is perfectly adapted to a particular habitat. Division into five super-families (which group the 12 families now in existence) is probably the best solution.

Bush rats, tuco-tucos (p. 2602), rat-chinchillas, porcupine-rats, hutia (p. 1279) and spiny rats form the first super-family; viscacha (p. 2640) and chinchilla (p. 562) the second; cavies (p. 1126), Patagonian hares (p. 1126), capybaras (p. 504), agouti (p. 61) and paca (p. 1802) the third. Pacaranas (p.

1802) constitute a family of their own, and the three-spined porcupine is given its own sub-family.

Rodents are widely distributed over all South America in quite well determined regions, which vary according to the lifestyles of the creatures concerned. Patagonian hares (genus *Dolichotis*) are found on open plains. Tuco-tucos live in deserts on high plateaus. The viscacha, or pampas hare *Lagostomus maximus*, is perfectly acclimatized to the great dry plains of the pampas. Agoutis happily live in quite different habitats–humid forest, dry forest or clear savanna.

Coatis provide a good example of the adaptive faculty and the South American coati *Nasua nasua* (p..592) with a dozen sub-species is no exception. A group of coatis will effectively clean up a good area of steppe, and then move on.

South American carnivores

Grison (*Galictis*) have a similar function in South America to that of western polecats, both being mustelids. The potto, or kinkajou *Potos flavus* (p. 1369) lives in tropical forest and this single species is a member of the family Procyonidae, the raccoon group.

There are seven species of canid found in South America. The grey fox *Urocyon cinereoargenteus* (p. 1099) is a North American species which lives as far south as Northern Colombia and Venezuela, where it adapts to all environments. Some authorities regard the North and South American varieties as two distinct species. The crab-eating fox *Cerdocyon thous* (p. 690) lives from Colombia to Uruguay and will leave forest to venture on to thicketed plains. The small-eared fox or zorro *Atelocynus microtis* (p. 2802), whose ways in the wild are little known, prefers to live in the great dense forests of Venezuela, Colombia and the Amazon.

The bushdog *Speothus venaticus* (p. 463) passes with ease from forest to arboreal steppe and can be found from northern Panama to Bolivia. Its genealogy is a subject of debate. The various foxes of the genus *Dusicyon* divide the south of the continent between them. The colpeo, or Magellan wolf *D. culpaeus* has its habitat in the sparse forest and desert plains of Tierra del Fuego and Patagonia, as well as near the Andes right up to the Equator. It owes this geographical

versatility to its diet of rodents, birds and lizards. The pampas fox *D. gymnocercus* shares some of its territory with the Azara fox *D. azarae* (p. 1534). From valley to barren regions, they clean up the pampas and can be met at high altitude as well. The Brazil hoary fox *Lycalopes vetulus* lives on the 'campos', the empty savanna of Brazil. The maned wolf *Chrysocyon brachyurus* (p. 1534) occupies a slightly larger, but quite as central, territory as the Brazil fox—consisting of Brazil, eastern Bolivia, Paraguay and northern Argentina.

The cats

The family Felidae is also represented in South America. The margay *Leopardus wiedi*, an excellent climber, is one. The ocelot *L. pardalis* (p. 1742) is well known and the little tiger-cat *L. tigrinus*—which is no larger than a small domestic cat—is widely spread through Latin America.

Geoffroy's cat *L. geoffroyi* is ranked, with the ocelot, among smaller South American felines. It lives in dry regions in the south of Bolivia, Paraguay and Uruguay, and in

Argentina up to the region of Patagonia.

The little kodkol (*L. guigna*), which is generally a forest-dweller in the foothills of the Andes in Chile, also enters open, though always bushy, regions.

The pampas cat

The pampas cat *Lynchailurus pajeros* has a hairy look to it on account of its stiff and lustreless coat. (In general individuals of the southern regions of Argentina and Chile tend to grow extra-thick coats.) The pampas cat shows how widely a species can be distributed. For it is found from the Andes region of the Equator right down to southern Patagonia—and along with Geoffroy's cat, is the most southern feline in the world. In Argentina, Uruguay, Paraguay, the extreme south of Brazil and middle Chile, it lives on the plains. But in central and northern Chile, Bolivia, Peru and Ecuador, it is an inhabitant of temperate mountainous regions. It is never found in forests and avoids humid tropical zones.

The pampas cat is common on the great grassy plains of Patagonia near the Magellan

The mountain viscacha Lagidium peruanum, *sometimes called the mountain chinchilla, is smaller than its plains relative and lives in rocky crevices in the Andes of Peru, Bolivia and Argentina.*

Straits. This cat is said to live close to pools surrounded by high grass in the low-lying regions of Uruguay. Throughout the Argentine it likes relatively wet pampas and 'pajonales' where the little mammals it feeds on—such as cavies, partridge and quail—abound.

In Ecuador, however, the pampas cat has been found in a field of sugar-cane near Quito at an altitude of 6000 ft, while in the plains to the south of Buenos Aires it shelters in regions with tatou and viscacha.

The Andes cat *Oreailurus jacobita* and the jaguarundi *Herpailurus yagouaroundi* (p. 1319) remain in forests and wooded savanna.

Though we spoke of the puma *Felis concolor* (p. 2009) in relation to North America, it also extends through the southern continent—as far south as Patagonia. A versatile animal, it seems as much at home in the tropical forests of Brazil as it is on the Argentinian pampas.

'El tigre'

Known as 'el tigre' (the tiger) in South America, the jaguar *Panthera onca* (p. 1315) is the largest of the American cats—and one of the most widespread; it can be seen from the south of the United States right down to the Argentine. The jaguar is adapted to forest, bush, plain, and high grass. It needs only cover, as it hunts on the ground.

South American reptiles

Certain archaic reptiles are only found in wooded and steppe country. Others, like the Peruvian iguana, can live at very high altitudes. Caiman (p. 483) are distributed from Central America to the middle of South America. The genus has two species: the spectacled or South American caiman *Caiman crocodilus* and the wide-jawed caiman *C. latirostris*. At 15 ft, the black caiman *Melanosuchus niger* is twice the size of either of these and is hunted assiduously. The pygmy caiman (*Paleosuchus* spp) is a tough little creature and is found in the centre of the continent.

The gecko *Hermidactylus mabouia* came (probably on boats) to South America from Africa at a relatively recent time. All the same, this species has spread throughout the upper part of the continent and even penetrated along the rivers of Brazil. Rather surprisingly, skinks of the genus *Mabuya* are also found in the New World. Some experts are prepared to believe they arrived on floating wood all the way from Africa; others think they came from Asia via the Bering Isthmus—which is a long way from Argentina.

Many South American lizards go by the name of teiid or tegu, and the family Teiidae is exclusively American (p. 2495). The family is represented in North America by the racerunners and whiptails, such as the dotted whiptail *Cnemidophorus lemniscatus*, which is a species that has penetrated South America. Other members of the family are well distributed in the South; for example,

Resting in the shade, a jaguar Panthera onca *waits for its prey.*

the three-toed tegu *Teius teyou* in southern Brazil and Argentina and the desert tegu *Dicrodon* in Peru.

Tegus of the genus *Tupinambis* are often cited, as they are the largest of all. The hen-house tegu *T. nigropunctatus* is found in Central America and northern South America, as is the common or bodyguard tegu *T. teguixin*. The red tegu *T. rufescens* lives in Argentina. These lizards vary in length between 4 ft and 4½ ft.

The worst enemy of the little desert tegus of Peru is a member of their own family – the yard-long false monitor *Tejovaranus flavipunctatus* – which eats them. Teiids which live in or near water include the caiman lizard *Dracaena guianensis*, which lives in marshy forest to the north-east of South America, and the lizard-crocodiles *Crocodilurus lacertinus* of Central America and northern South America.

Aquatic tegus are widely distributed in numerous species, some of them little known and although they are grouped together, they are not all essentially aquatic. The streamlined tegu *Neusticurus bicarinatus* is the most dependent on water. The spectacled tegus of the genus *Gymnophthalmus* have transparent eyelids and live well hidden. Pygmy tegus are grouped in five genera with a dozen species. The thorny tegu *Echinosaura horrida* of Panama, Colombia and Ecuador, will feign death when danger threatens. The lizards of the genus *Anadia* are arboreal.

Birds of the pampas

South America has a southerly and wide-reaching climatic 'balcony' and becomes appreciably colder after the Tropic of Capricorn. As a result, there are considerable differences in its landscape between the Patagonian desert steppe, pampas proper, *monte* or dry bush – and *chaco* or dry bushy forest.

The pampas brings to mind gauchos and great herds of cattle. But it is still a true land of wild creatures which can accommodate themselves to the rare presence of man. The rhea (p. 2080) is one of these. Symbolic of the pampas and sometimes called the ostrich of the New World, Darwin's rhea *Pterocnemia pennata* lives on the high plateaus of the

The broad-snouted caiman. Caimans differ from crocodiles and alligators in having very large overlapping bony plates in their bellies.

Zani – Vendal – Jacana

116

Andes; while the common American rhea *Rhea americana* avoids mountains and forests and is found on uncultivated plains.

There are nine genera of tinamous (p. 2534) evenly spread throughout South America and over 40 species. Zoologists class tinamous in two great sub-families: the Tinaminae which live in forest; and the Rhynchotinae of the steppes. The major difference between them is the placing of their nostrils. Forest tinamous have them in the middle of their beaks; steppe species at their base.

Herons and flamingoes

Herons of different species can be found virtually everywhere in the world. A South American member of the genus *Ardea* is the sokoi heron *A. cocoi* (p. 1191). The great or large white egret *Egretta alba* (p. 828) lives in the New World as well as the Old, and America has its own egret, the snowy egret *E. thula*.

The three-coloured heron *Hydranassa tricolor* lives in colonies which number thousands of members; the boat-billed heron or boatbill *Cochlearius cochlearius* (p. 388) is found in tropical America, and the whistling heron *Syrigma sibilatrix* in the south of Brazil and Argentina. The bilhoreau *Pilherodius pileatus* nests in Panama and tropical America.

Among the tiger herons, a primitive group, are several species of heron which many specialists class with the bittern sub-family (p. 359). Small bitterns of the genus *Ixobrychus* are called blongios. The little bittern *Ixobrychus exilis* is the smallest species of heron in existence, while large bitterns, of the genus *Botaurus*, have a tail twice as long as that of most South American bitterns. An endemic bittern which is typically South American is the pinnated bittern *Botaurus pinnatus*.

Pink flamingoes *Phoenicopterus ruber* (p. 922) can be found as far south as Tierra del Fuego, though Chile and the Andes have some species of their own. The white-faced ibis *Plegadis chihi* has a strange distribution, being firmly rooted in both Americas—though not in large regions. South America

The common or bodyguard tegu Tupinambis teguixin. *The female sometimes lays her eggs in termite nests, where they will definitely be safe.*

Y. Vial – Jacana

has several species of ibis, including the blue ibis *Harpipron caerulescens*, the white-necked ibis *Theristicus caudatus* and related forms. The American roseate spoonbill *Ajaja ajaja* (p. 2358) has the same pigmentation as flamingoes.

Water birds

South America has an impressive number of ducks and waterfowl of the order Anseriformes. The screamers (p. 2171) of the family Anhimidae include the crested screamer *Chauna torquata*, which lives in marshy regions of the pampas, the horned screamer *Anhima cornuta* of the Amazon forest and the black-necked screamer *C. chavaria*, which lives on the banks of forested rivers in Venezuela and Colombia. One species of swan endemic to South America is the coscoroba swan *Coscoroba coscoroba* (p. 2448), which has white plumage and red feet and is the smallest of described forms. It may be related to the whistling ducks. The black-necked swan *Cygnus melanocoryphus* winters in the south of Chile and in Tierra del Fuego.

Ducks of the sub-family Anatinae are well represented in South America. Sheldrake and the goose-like grazing duck of the genus *Chloephaga* are sub-divided according to regions – with certain species living in flocks on the plains. But the Andes goose *Chloephaga melanoptera* lives where its name suggests. Barnacle geese of the same genus live to the south of the continent; the ashy-headed individual goes from southern Chile to the Magellan Straits. Ruddy-headed, upland or Magellan and Antarctic geese are all of the same genus and are all confined to the south as well.

Steamer ducks (p. 2386) of the genus *Tachyeres* are also worth mentioning, as two of the three species are unable to fly. The Andes crested sheldrake *Lophonetta speculariodes* is considered an intermediary breed. The brightly coloured pink-beaked duck *Netta peposaca* (p. 1938) is a fine South American representative of the pochards. The muscovy duck *Cairina moschata* (p. 1683) is a descendant of the greylag goose (p. 1101), which itself has long been domesticated. In wooded regions of South America one can even find perching ducks, with long strong claws that allow them to roost and nest in trees.

In general, the tapaculo is a bird peculiar to bushy steppe and it lives comfortably on the thorny bushes of certain areas of the pampas. But there are 26 species of tapaculo – and all have slightly different habitats. One, known as the 'embankment bird' digs out burrows in the raised earth bordering roads. Others build cunningly hidden nests low in bushes. Tapaculos are members of the family Rhinocryptidae and are secretive birds – there is as yet a great deal unknown about them.

Both on land and in water, the South American plains have a wealth of all sorts of invertebrates for their bird fauna to feed on. In both running and still waters there are numerous worms and insects, as well as molluscs and crustaceans. Locusts, grasshoppers, mantids and cockroaches abound on the prairie, where flies and mosquitoes swarm. Some tiny insects even live on the birds themselves, and these parasites can carry diseases which afflict imported animals.

South American bats

Vampire bats (p. 2625) – the only parasitic mammals – are limited to Central and South America. They bite sleeping mammals and birds and feed on their blood, and in the process can transmit rabies and other diseases. Belonging to the family Desmodontidae (of the sub-order Microchiroptera), vampire bats are not the only bats present in the southern continent, but they are the only true bats that feed on blood. The common vampire *Desmodus rotundus* is the most widespread, while the other two species, the white-winged vampire *Diaemus youngi* and the hairy-legged vampire *Diphylla ecaudata*, are essentially tropical, and little is known about them.

One family of bats, which is usually called fer-de-lance, should not be confused with the reptiles of the same name. These Phyllos-

Black-necked swans Cygnus melanocoryphus *are found from Brazil to Tierra del Fuego and the Falkland Islands.*

tomidae live in hot regions of America. The naked-backed bat, genus *Pteronotus*, only penetrates as far south as northern South America, but abounds in Central America. The javelin false vampire bat (*Vampyrum spectrum*) does not deserve its Latin name, for it does not suck blood.

There are two species of Mexico bulldog-bat or fish-eating bat (p. 919) in South America. One is the hare-lipped *Noctilio leporinus* which feeds exclusively on fish, of which South America has the richest supply in the world.

South American fish
South American fish number some 2000 species, the majority of them found in major river systems like the Orinoco, Amazon, Paran and Paraguay. Their variety is extraordinary – ranging from piranha, cat-fish and venomous rays, to the South American lungfish *Lepidosiren paradoxa* (p. 1484) which, in a dry season, tunnels into the river mud to survive – and seems to be impervious to pollution.

There are some 600 numbered species of cichlids (p. 574) in the world (and probably more that have not yet been discovered). They resemble perch, but only have a single nostril on each side of their heads (perch have two). Angelfish or scalare *Pterophyllum* (p. 2152) live in the waters of the Amazon, the spectacular firemouth cichlid *Cichlasoma*

meeki (p. 914) in Central America. The southern land has many other species of the same genus; the best known are probably the greenish black 'Jack Dempsey' boxer-fish *C. biocellatum* (p. 1311) and the magnificent pompadour or discus *Symphysodon discus* (p. 1953) of the Amazon, which resembles the beautiful butterfly fish of tropical coral seas.

Fish and continental drift
The arapaima *Arapaima gigas* belongs to the order Osteoglossiformes which as genera are distributed in three major regions of the world: South America, Africa and Australia, and in each continent the fish are found in clearly delimited zones. All have prominent scales, large eyes and bony plates on the head. The arapaima is one of the largest freshwater fish in existence. It has different names in each of its countries and in Brazil is known as picarucu. The arawana *Osteoglossum bicirrhosum* of the same order lives in the same region.

The South American leaf-fish *Monocirrhus polyacanthus* (p. 1421) is also found in Africa and in India where it is known as *Badis badis*. Again, Australian trout (Galaxiidae) are found in three southern areas – Australia, Africa and South America. The American species, the galaxid *Galaxias maculatus* is found from Chile southwards – and some palaeontologists believe this indicates the existence of a continent to the south of South

America in the far distant past.

Fish of the family Characidae are found nowhere else in the world apart from tropical and sub-tropical Africa and America. There are a great many other species that the two continents have in common, which would seem to confirm the theory of Continental Drift. But it is also worth remembering that, starting from a common structure, fish have a considerable faculty for adaptation (as exemplified by the fact that so many can reproduce in aquaria) and, whatever their species, experience the evolutionary process to the full.

In the family Myleindae, the genera *Mylossoma* and *Myloplus* have the elegance of piranha, but lack their voraciousness and are vegetarians. In contrast, American characins are almost all carnivorous and members of the genus *Agoniates*, which live in the large rivers of Guyana and in the Amazon, feed on other fish. South American waters in fact are full of surprises. *Rhaphiodon gibbus* resembles a deep-sea fish; the genera *Astynax* and *Anoptichthys* (p. 535) are blind; the hatchet-fish, *Gasteropelecus* and *Carnegiella* (p. 1175) can flap themselves up out of the water and effectively fly across its surface using their pectoral fins. (Other so-called 'flying' fish – the marine fish *Exocoetus* (p. 946) and the fresh water butterfly fish *Pantodon* (p. 471) – actually glide.)

The piranha (p. 1915) is, of course, notori-

The common vampire bat feeds only on the fresh blood of mammals and birds. Its saliva contains substances that prevent blood from clotting.

ous and other flesh-eaters, such as the *Oligosarcus* and the *Acestrorhynchus*, are hardly less voracious. In silhouette they look like pike and vary in length from 8 to 12 in. Others resemble herrings and for this reason are known as Clupeacharacinae. All the fish of this immense sub-order have some peculiarity. Glandulocaudinae, for instance, reproduce in a special manner, with their eggs being fertilized internally and then laid by the female a good deal later. Another member of the family, the *Corynopoma riisei*, has an appendage with which it attracts the female of the species. All these fish are adapted to surface waters and have enlarged pectoral fins.

Electric fish and catfish

Electric eels or gymnotids, which are also known as knife-fish because of their flat and pointed bodies, are active at night. There are 15 genera of the family Electrophoridae. They live in waters of the low regions of Central and tropical America, and their bare cylindrical bodies can grow to considerable sizes. The electric eel *Electrophorus electricus* (p. 839) is given a wide berth by other creatures and is seldom attacked. As a result, it does not have to regenerate itself as much as other gymnotids, which all have the extraordinary ability to replace parts of their body—such as damaged tails, scales, fins and muscles.

South America has the world's largest contingent of Siluriformes—in fact, more than half of their 2000 species. Catfish are part of this order. They owe their name to the barbels on their jaws, and those of the genus *Ictalurus* are found in North America. The family Pimelodidae is the richest in terms of genera in South America. It includes *Rhamdia sebae*, which grows to 15 in. long and has impressive barbels (one pair of which reach its caudal fin), the cat-fish *Sorubim lima*, which has an upper jaw that is considerably longer than its lower, *Pseudoplatystoma fasciatum*, which has a head like the beak of a duck, and the little (3 in.) bumble-bee catfish *Microglanis Parahybae*.

The red piranha Serrasalmus nattereri. *It jaws are strong and its teeth are very sharp and it can chop out a piece of flesh very neatly.*

Serge Pecolatto – Jacana

The family Trichomycteridae is another South American group of catfish, so thin one could consider them worms. Some of them are perfect parasites, and the candiru, of the genus *Vandellia*, is even a parasite on man, entering the urogenital systems of bathers.

The family Callichthyidae are often seen in aquaria. In their natural state they live in large shoals in the central waters of the continent and like to stay where currents are weaker at the bottom, as they are not strong swimmers. The catfish of the genera *Corydoras* (p. 178) and *Brochis* use their barbels to catch hold of particles of food.

The armoured catfish of the family Loricariidae (p. 178) are covered with bony plates reminiscent of armour. They have strongly differentiated river habitats and one finds them in the most unexpected places. The largest of the family, *Plecostomus*, grows to 3 ft long, and is capable of climbing the swiftest-flowing watercourses as far as their sources in the Andes.

Pterygoblichtys is gifted with pectoral fins that look as if they are wings. The smooth-armoured catfish *Loricaria* digs itself into soft river bottoms, where it lies with only its eyes showing above the mud. The twig catfish of the genus *Farlowella* are characterized by their long beak-shaped appendages. These appendages are used to scrape algae and other minute plant life from rocks and the bed of the river in which they live.

The four-eyed fish *Anableps anableps* (p. 967) is the only member of its family, the Anablepidae. It spends its time floating right at the surface of the water. The structure of its eyes conforms to this life-style—and the crystalline lens of its eyes has a horizontal partition that allows it to see as well in the air as in the water. The male has a scaly tube-shaped reproductive organ on its anal fin. There are many other equally strange South American fish, such as the upside-down catfish *Synodontis nigriventris*, which feeds on the surface by swimming on its back. Its belly is dark and its back is light—the opposite of normal fish camouflage.

The electric eel Electrophorus electricus. *The electric shock, with which it kills its food, is strong enough to kill a horse.*

△ *The mailed catfish* Calichthys calichthys *is heavily armoured and can travel overland using strong spines.*

▽ *Morphos are among the largest and most beautiful of butterflies. There are less than 50 species, ranging from central Mexico to southern Brazil.*

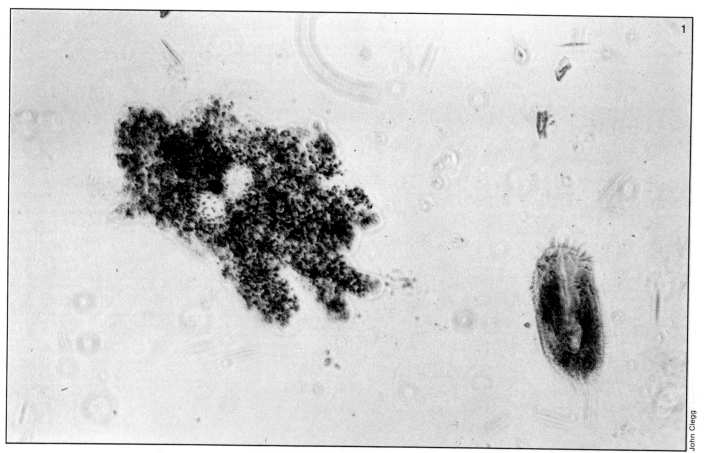

John Clegg

Amoeba

Amoebae form a group of the single-celled organisms called Protozoa. Protozoa means 'first animals', and as these organisms have affinities with plants, some of them photosynthesise.

Like any cell the amoeba consists basically of an envelope containing the substance protoplasm. *In the middle of the cell, surrounded by the protoplasm, is the* nucleus, *a body which can be thought of as a blueprint for the organisation of the cell's activities. If an amoeba is cut in two the half with the nucleus may survive and reproduce; the other moves around for a while but cannot digest its food, and when its reserves are gone it dies.*

The protoplasm is not, as was once thought, a jelly; it has a very complicated structure, and consists of a cytoplasm divided into a granular endoplasm and at the ends of the pseudopodia, and elsewhere under the surface, a clearer layer known as ectoplasm.

Many amoebae

The name amoeba is applied not only to members of the genus *Amoeba* but to a range of different types of Protozoa with pseudopodia (see below) living in the sea, in fresh water, in damp soil and in the bodies of larger animals. They include some with shells, like *Arcella*, and also the half-dozen species that live in the human mouth and digestive system, one of which is the cause of amoebic dysentery *(Entamoeba)*. Some amoebae contain many nuclei, among them the giant *Chaos carolinensis*, which may measure up to $\frac{1}{5}$ in.

Amoeba proteus, the textbook amoeba, measuring about $\frac{1}{50}$ in., is just visible to the naked eye and may be found in fairly still fresh water. It moves about by extending a finger of protoplasm, called a pseudopodium ('false foot'). As the pseudopodium enlarges, the cell contents—protoplasm and nucleus—flow into it, while the rest of the cell contracts behind. Though it has no definite shape, the amoeba is not a shapeless sac of protoplasm, for it has a permanent hind end and forms its pseudopodium in a characteristic pattern according to the species.

Feeding

The amoeba feeds on other Protozoa. It does so by 'flowing' around them, the protoplasm completely surrounding the food to enclose it in a 'food vacuole' containing fluid in which the prey was swimming. Digestion is a similar process to that occurring in many other organisms: digestive juices are secreted into the food vacuole and the digestible parts are broken down and absorbed. The rest is merely left behind as the amoeba moves along.

This process is known as phagocytosis, from the Greek 'eating by cells'. In a similar process called pinocytosis, or 'drinking by cells', channels are formed from the cell surface, leading into the cell. Fluid is drawn into the channels and from their tips vacuoles are pinched off. The fluid is then absorbed into the protoplasm in the same way as the digested contents of the food vacuoles. This is a method of absorbing fluids in bulk into the cell.

Water is continually passing in through the cell membrane as well as being brought in by phagocytosis and pinocytosis. Excess is pumped out by contractile vacuoles which fill with water and then collapse, discharging the water to the outside.

Reproduction

The amoeba reproduces itself by dividing into two equal parts, a process known as binary fission and taking less than an hour. It begins with the amoeba becoming spherical. The nucleus divides into two, and the two halves move apart and the cell then splits down the middle.

Amoeba proteus seemingly reproduces only by binary fission but other species may reproduce in a different manner. In binary fission the nucleus divides into hundreds of small ones and each becomes surrounded by a little cytoplasm and a tough wall—all within the original cell. The resulting 'cysts' can survive if the water dries up and can be dispersed to found new populations. Larger cysts may be formed without reproduction taking place, when the whole cell surrounds itself with a thick wall. Though some amoebae reproduce sexually, *Amoeba proteus* has never been seen to do so.

Pushing or pulling?

The story of the amoeba illustrates not only the advances made in the last few decades in the techniques of microscopy but also the difficulties involved in research.

Years ago microscopists could watch amoeba only from above in the usual manner of looking at very small objects. From this angle one could see the pseudo-

Popular protozoan

1 (overleaf) The well-known one-celled animal, amoeba, showing large water excreting vacuoles. This picture includes a Stylonychian, which belongs to another, ciliated, group of protozoans. (Magnified 150 times).
2 Amoeboid movement—streaming of the cytoplasm can be clearly seen.
3 Diagram of modern microscope's side view of amoeba moving to the right on small protoplasmic pegs with pseudopodium, or false-foot, extended.
4 Amoeba with nucleus, which controls cell, divided, prior to cell splitting into two.
5 Special light phase contrast microscope gives this beautiful view of amoeba showing food in vacuoles.

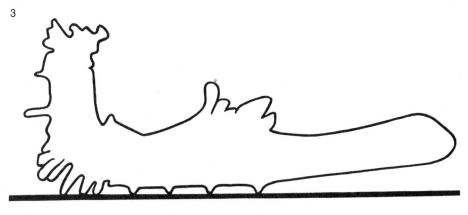

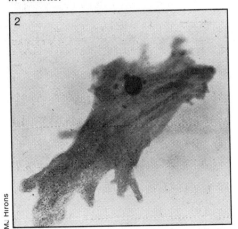

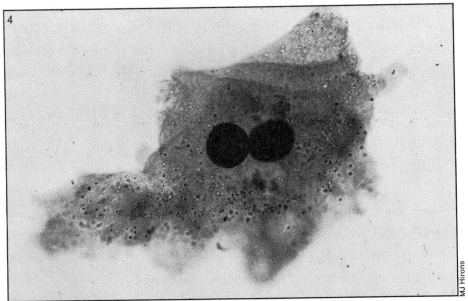

podia advancing over the surface of the microscope slide and apparently in contact with it. Recently, however, a technique has been devised for watching it from the side and a new detail has come to light. In fact, when each pseudopodium moves forward it is supported by an extremely small peg of protoplasm which remains attached to the ground at one spot while the rest of the animal, raised just above the ground, advances over it. Finally, the pseudopodium is withdrawn and reincorporated into the body of the amoeba.

A number of theories of 'amoeboid movement' have been proposed over the last 20 years but its mechanism is still not thoroughly understood. One can see, under the higher powers of the microscope, the protoplasm streaming forwards along the centre of the pseudopodium and moving out to the sides at the tip in what has been descriptively named the 'fountain zone', and there acquiring a firmer consistency. At the same time the reverse change occurs at the 'tail', where the protoplasm resumes its forward flow.

What is still in doubt is whether the advancing protoplasm is being pushed forward from behind, like toothpaste in its tube, or pulled by changes in the proteins in the fountain zone. The problem is by no means trivial, for some of our own cells move in an amoeboid manner and its solution in terms of the behaviour of protein molecules could cast light on one of the basic properties of protoplasm.

phylum	**Protozoa**
class	**Sarcodina**
order	**Lobosa**

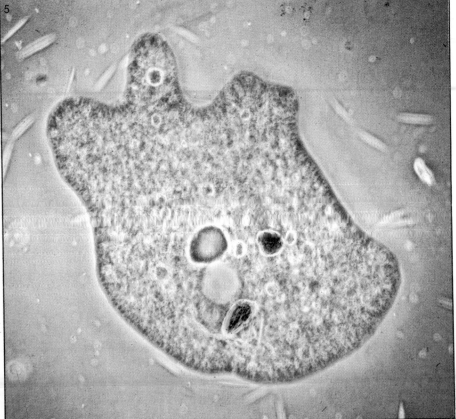